BRITISH-AMERICAN DIPLOMACY 1895-1917

Early Years of the Special Relationship

David H. Burton

Professor of History
Saint Joseph's University

AN ANVIL ORIGINAL
under the general editorship of
Hans L. Trefousse

KRIEGER PUBLISHING COMPANY
MALABAR, FLORIDA
1999

Original Edition 1999

Printed and Published by
KRIEGER PUBLISHING COMPANY
KRIEGER DRIVE
MALABAR, FLORIDA 32950

Copyright © 1999 by David H. Burton

Library of Congress Cataloging-In-Publication Data

Burton, David Henry, 1925–
     British-American diplomacy, 1895–1917 : early years of the special relationship / David H. Burton.
         p.   cm. — (The Anvil series)
     "An Anvil original."
     Includes bibliographical references and index.
     ISBN 1-57524-048-3 (pbk. : alk. paper)
     1. United States—Foreign relations—Great Britain.   2. Great Britain—Foreign relations—United States.   3. United States—Foreign relations—1865–1921.   I. Title.
E183.8.G7B94   1999
327.41073—dc21   98-24924
                                                    CIP

10   9   8   7   6   5   4   3   2

For
Nicholas David

THE ANVIL SERIES

Anvil paperbacks give an original analysis of a major field of history or a problem area, drawing upon the most recent research. They present a concise treatment and can act as supplementary material for college history courses. Written by many of the outstanding historians in the United States, the format is one-half narrative text, one-half supporting documents, often from hard to find sources.

CONTENTS

PART I—British American Diplomacy 1895–1917

PART II—Documents

CONTENTS

PART I

BRITISH-AMERICAN DIPLOMACY 1895–1917

INTRODUCTION

The years between 1895 and 1917 witnessed a most remarkable about-face in the conduct of British diplomacy, and consequently, of how the United States was to come to understand and appreciate Great Britain's support and encouragement of America's world pretensions. Due to a considerable measure this new friendship between the two great English-speaking nations, the new century was on its way to become the American century. These two factors, London's search for a new foreign policy of global proportions and Washington's striving to be recognized as a great power, were inextricably linked. Great Britain stood at the zenith of her power. For decades virtually unchallenged as the mightiest of empires Britain and her Foreign Office professionals might well scoff at the idea that the American republic would soon be a critical component in her grand diplomatic strategy. Americans, to be sure, continued to nurse old grudges toward the erstwhile mother country. Not only the immigrant Irish but the Boston brahmin, Henry Cabot Lodge among them, found the British lion's tail something to be twisted whenever the occasion warranted. Still, it must be remembered that in the 1890s Brittania ruled the waves and the United States navy was not highly ranked. The sun never set on the Union Jack while the Stars and Stripes fluttered over American Samoa. British ministers were recognized statesmen, their American equivalents all too likely to be neophytes, particularly in the field of diplomacy. In sum, relations between the two nations appeared to remain on course, dictated more by reason of British power than by American ambition, only to have a dispute over a boundary line between British Guiana and Venezuela set in motion events that would give a new look to British–American diplomacy.

As is invariably the case with historical and historic change the Anglo-American special relationship was the outgrowth of an intersection of men and events, events over which the men involved did not have full control, but the men themselves were, by their policies and actions, crucial to the outcome.

At first glance events appear to have been the controlling factor as Great Britain and the United States prepared to forget old animosities or to forebear, as new controversies arose. Chief among these was the

3

coming of age of the new Germany. Under Otto von Bismarck's leadership the German nation was Euro-centered; in the Iron Chancellor's view colonies "were not the worth the bones of a Pomeranian grenadier." In 1890 the young Kaiser, Wilhelm II, removed Bismarck from office and from influence in affairs of state, proposing to seek an imperial destiny for his proud nation. In keeping with the dictum of the American geopolitician, A. T. Mahan, greatness for Germany rested to a large extent on a large navy. Such a force would be crucial in winning and keeping colonies in Africa or in the far Pacific, and perhaps in the Americas. The Kaiser was also impressed by the writings of Houston S. Chamberlain whose "heartland" thesis led planners to think in terms of wielding power from Berlin to Baghdad. This strategy, combining sea and land elements, should it materialize, would be a direct challenge not alone to the Royal Navy but it would also pose a threat to Suez and the lifeline to India. Such developments London could not tolerate. Germany began to look more and more like a threat to British hegemony.

Was the end of Britain's "splendid isolation" at hand? And if so should not the Foreign Office begin to mature plans to gain allies whose interests were also at risk should German ambitions go unchecked? Quite apart from any new relationship with the United States, which initially did not hold obvious promise, London and Paris agreed on an understanding, the Entente Cordiale in 1904. Three years thereafter the Triple Entente: Britain, France, and Russia came into being. A meaningful friendship with America, should it come to pass, would solidify Great Britain's defensive alliance system and enable it to maintain the status quo. Furthermore the Anglo-Japanese treaty, that seemed secondary at the time of its signing, 1902, was indication of London's well thought-out *weltpolitik*. The understandings with Paris, St. Petersburg, and Tokyo were formal treaties but no such arrangements was likely with the United States. Instead, perhaps a rapprochement based on an identity of interests and drawing on the common bonds of language, literature and law, could be managed. In the United States this would not be inconsistent with President Washington's advice against entangling alliances and would ensure American neutrality in any future war among the Old World powers.

In the United States forces were at work well below the surface events, impulses that would shortly both cause and explain America's quick entry into world politics. Navalism, Social Darwinism, commercialism, and patriotism were congealing to shape and texture a vibrant nationalism. But where would this New World nation fit in the patterns of competing empires that were themselves dangerously nationalistic? The Monroe Doctrine, announced as long ago as 1823, was the center piece of American foreign policy. Pertaining to the western hemisphere it delivered a warning to potential interlopers: "Hands off!" European colonization or re-colonization was expressly singled out. By the 1890s the Doctrine had become cut in stone. It appeared unlikely that any European country would be prepared to defy its major premise, but with Germany in an expansive mood there was no outright assurance of that. Ironically it was what the Americans would perceive as a violation by the British of the Monroe Doctrine in an 1895 dispute between Venezuela and Britain over a boundary line which was to lead on to a detente embraced by both Washington and London. This accord was significantly strengthened by British support for the United States when war broke out with Spain in 1898. Though there were disagreements thereafter between the two countries on small but not unimportant matters, for example, the Alaskan boundary dispute in 1903, an informal alliance, a quasi-entente, had come into being. It reached a climax in 1917 when the United States entered World War I as an associated power, joining with England and France in what President Wilson was to call the war to end all wars. Mention of Woodrow Wilson is a reminder that, after all, it was a mix of men and events that gave birth to the special relationship, men who nurtured it in its infancy and who continued to promote it, and events, such as Germany's decision to return to unrestricted submarine warfare at the start of 1917, which rendered Wilson's neutrality policy an impossible dream. Who then were the leaders, Wilson among them, whose sense of history and of world order gave rise to policies shaping the early years of the special relationship?

It would be a mistake to single out the men who favored the relationship as in any way its architects. There was no grand design, no blueprint the product of one mind or more, either in London or Washington. No doubt the vision was there in the work of someone like James Bryce who in *The American Commonwealth* assumed the common bonds found in law and government could well bring about an alliance one day. Among the British statesmen who contributed directly to the formation of the relationship mention must be made of the Marquess of Salisbury who was for some years both prime minister and foreign secretary, Joseph Chamberlain, the colonial secretary under Salisbury, Lord Lansdowne, foreign secretary in the Balfour government, Sir Edward

Grey who succeeded Lansdowne, under both Campbell-Bannerman and Asquith. At a more junior level Sir Cecil Spring Rice, a close friend of Theodore Roosevelt and His Majesty's (HM) ambassador to Washington during World War I and Arthur Hamilton Lee (Viscount Lee of Fareham) a subcabinet minister and another friend of TR, had influence well beyond that commensurate with their positions. Other English advocates of a warm friendship with the United States in addition to Lord Bryce were St. Loe Strachey, editor of *The Spectator* and the distinguished historian, Sir George Otto Trevelyan.

The single most outspoken American champion of Anglo-American cooperation was Theodore Roosevelt, before, during and after his presidency. He had plenty of high ranking company, Secretary of State John Hay, Secretary of War and later of State, Elihu Root, and William Howard Taft while in the Roosevelt cabinet and later as president. In the later years Woodrow Wilson's predilections were strongly pro-British as were those of Colonel House, Wilson's alter ego, and Walter Hines Page the American ambassador to London.

Again it must be stressed that leaders alone did not bring the two nations together. Rather, events, differently interpreted by the British and the Americans, were such as to enable them to perceive a common peril and to act in concert to meet it. The relationship was not a contrivance. It derived instead from the response of like-minded peoples and nations in which each country was determined to protect its own interests. This was possible because there was no deep-seated clash of priorities. By 1917 men and events had amply demonstrated that national self-interest need not be divisive. If the fundamental values of the two peoples were alike, if their histories had much in common, if their institutions enjoyed a nurturing kinship, and if their man in the street saw much to admire in each other without yielding criticism to friendship, then national self-interest in times of crisis no less than in times of calm, became a mutual self-interest. In the diplomatic world of the early twentieth century only the Anglo-Americans were to know and to profit from such accord. What follows is an account of how the special relationship came about, why it was able to survive the tests to which it was put, and finally the triumph of the very idea of England and America coming together to fight a common foe. And it is necessary only to allude to the decisive place the working alliance of the United States and Great Britain was to have in the winning of World War II. British-American diplomacy, 1895-1917, should be thought of as dealing with a watershed period for much of international politics in this century.

CHAPTER 1

UNCERTAIN BEGINNINGS

A Twenty-Inch Gun. The official quiet of the British foreign office was shattered suddenly, and from an unexpected quarter, by a note delivered by the American ambassador, Thomas F. Bayard, in late July 1895. President Grover Cleveland likened it to the firing of a "twenty-inch gun." The author of the salvo was the Secretary of State Richard P. Olney. Newly appointed to his office, Olney was determined to bring to settlement a long standing dispute over the exact boundary line dividing Venezuelan territory from that of British Guiana. His draft note had been read and approved by the president. "It's the best thing of its kind I have ever read and it leads to a conclusion that one cannot escape if he tries—that is, if there is anything in the Monroe Doctrine at all," wrote Cleveland approvingly. And he went on: "You show there is a great deal in it and place it, I think, on better and more defensible ground than any of your predecessors or *mine*." The tone of the note made it the unhappy task for Ambassador Bayard, a moderate man by all accounts, to deliver it but as a responsible official he made no apology for what his government had asserted. Lord Salisbury, the prime minister, who also held the portfolio of foreign secretary was understandably taken aback. (*See Document No. 1.*)

At the outset the question needs to be posed: of what immediate business was it of the United States to involve itself in a boundary disagreement of long standing between two sovereign states? The answer comes swiftly to mind: the Cleveland administration was prepared to enlarge the scope of the Monroe Doctrine in response to what a neutral observer might find was the merest kind of British aggrandisement in the western hemisphere. The action the British proposed to take, namely to continue to insist that land long occupied by British subjects, hardly amounted to an invasion and indeed there had no resort to force by either party to the dispute. There was not a hint of gun boat diplomacy. What appeared to be gratuitous American interference in the matter had come with the suddenness of a summer storm. Whether it would pass as quickly could only be hoped.

A Boundary Line Is Drawn. The frontier demarcation in question had never been finalized from the time Venezuela had won its independence from Spain. As long ago as 1840 a British survey team led by Sir Robert Schomburgk had defined a tentative boundary line and invited the Venezuelans to accept its decision. Britain was willing to allow Point Barima, which controlled the entrance to the Orionoco River, to remain under Venezuelan jurisdiction in return for concessions in the interior. The effort proved to be a false start as Caracas took no final action regarding the Schomburgk line. In those days there appeared no urgency to come to agreement but there was a sense of frustration in London. Up to a point the lack of response from Caracas was understandable because of ongoing political instability in the country. When after 1876 gold was discovered in the interior, in the very areas the British had claimed as compensation for yielding on Point Barima, the issue of the boundary line flared up. Each side sought to make the most out of the confusion as claims and counterclaims went back and forth. The Venezuelan proposal to proceed to arbitration was rejected by Great Britain, largely on the grounds that a judgment would likely be rendered not on the merits of the case but by the habit of such commissions to split the disputed area between the two sides. In 1887 Caracas broke off diplomatic relations with Britain and appealed to the United States to act, largely on the grounds that the Monroe Doctrine was being threatened with violation by a non-American power. Nonetheless the State Department was not inclined to become involved, a policy determined by President Harrison's secretary of state, James G. Blaine, and that despite his reputation as "Jingo Jim." But the presidential office had changed hands and by 1893 Grover Cleveland was back in power. Because of incidents growing out of his failed reelection bid in 1888 he was more likely to look askance at the British claims than was Harrison. Even so, the situation might require the services of an *agent provocateur* were the United States to get fully involved.

Enter Mr. Scruggs. William L. Scruggs was to play such a role. A former United States minister to Caracas he had been removed from that position because he had bribed Venezuelan politicians, including the country's president. Back in the United States in 1894 Scruggs wrote an incendiary account of the troubles in Venezuela which were now beginning to smoulder, *British Aggression in Venezuela or The Monroe Doctrine On Trial*. The pamphlet was widely circulated among members of both houses of Congress as Scruggs had a useful contact in Representative Leonidas Livingston of Georgia. A joint resolution was passed, stating that arbitration was "earnestly recommended" as a way of settling the issue. The possible violation of the Monroe Doctrine figured directly in the thinking of both House and Senate. Congress seemed at this point to be taking the lead so that Cleveland and his first Secretary of State George Gresham were under some pressure to act, the more so because arrests were made by Venezuelan police of British subjects living in those areas where their settlements were long established. (*See Document No. 2.*)

Olney's Note. Gresham urged a moderate approach, but with his death in May 1895, he was succeeded by the more assertive Olney. The July 20 note, truculent in the extreme, made the following points. The honor of the government of the United States as well as its interests were central to the controversy. The Americas were in no part open to colonization, a proposition "long universally conceded." Whereupon Olney broadened his argument. "The rule in question has but a single purpose and object. It is that no European power or combination of European powers shall forcibly deprive an American state of the right and power of self-government and of shaping for itself its own political future and destiny." Rodomontade to be sure, and there was more to follow. "Today the United States is practically sovereign on this continent and its fiat is law upon subjects to which it confines its interposition." Such claims might well have led Salisbury to ponder his next move, the ball being clearly on his side of the net.

The prime minister was a seasoned diplomat and not likely to be moved to an equally excessive response. Calm, dispassionate, and ever on the lookout for British advantage as well as British prestige, Salisbury was determined to be patient, although a gauntlet had been thrown down. And ponder he did because he gauged the situation called for a measured attitude. A swift reply could only inflame American public opinion, he believed, whereas delay would give material interests time to offset "sentiments superficially held." Indeed, his whole manner was one of caution. Salisbury went so far as to warn the cabinet members that no one of them was to speak out in such a way as to agitate the American jingoes. His reason was that the American claim to the right to interfere in the boundary dispute was transparently ill advised. He further appreciated that neither Cleveland nor Olney were anti-British which, if they had been so, would have made defusing the troubling affair much more difficult. Thus it was that Salisbury waited four months, replying only in November 1895. This may well have been a tactical error. The absence of a rejoinder, what the jingoes had been hoping for, or even a routine response the administration waited for, was interpreted as another sign of British hauteur. Meanwhile the issue had continued to dominate the front pages of the metropolitan newspapers, especially on the east coast.

Salisbury's Reply. When Salisbury did reply he delivered what was a flat rejection of the American position. In language devoid of emotion, he made his government's stand unequivocal. Particular issue was taken with the proposition that the Monroe Doctrine was an accepted feature of international law. It must be borne in mind, Salisbury wrote, "international law is founded on the general consent of nations, and no statesman however eminent, and no nation, however powerful, are competent to insert into the code of international law a novel principle which was never recognized before and which has not since been accepted by the government of any country." The point at issue, the boundary dispute, Salisbury insisted had nothing to do with the Monroe Doctrine. London had spoken.

America Reacts. President Cleveland was greatly angered. In his reaction he appeared to give no consideration "to the unreliable character of the Venezuelan leaders and people, resulting in an almost indefensible, and therefore dangerous responsibility for the conduct of their affairs," the judgment offered by Ambassador Bayard in assessing the situation for the president. But Cleveland's indignation did not subside as he pushed for a show-down. "I am fully alive to the responsibility incurred, and keenly realize all the consequences of our policy" spelled out his frame of mind. On December 17 the president delivered an explosive message to congress. He testified that the claims of both sides had to be studied afresh, and called on congress to sanction the establishment of a commission to carry out a thorough investigation. And he warned that when the commission report was delivered it would be "the duty of the United States to resist by every means in its power as a willful act of aggression upon its rights and interests the appropriation by Great Britain of any lands or the exercise of any governmental jurisdiction over any territory which after investigation we have determined of right belongs to Venezuela." The funds were quickly voted to set up the commission which legislators and public alike believed would sweep away British claims. President Cleveland was above all else anti-imperi-alistic, an attitude which appeared to dominate his outlook in 1895. He had successfully derailed the move to annex the Hawaiian Islands in 1893 and that against powerful segments of the establishment. America simply could not be party to so unjust and indefensible an enterprise, whether in the Pacific or in South America. As far as the Monroe Doctrine was concerned Cleveland held firmly to the view that it was part of international law, the basis of international morality. Lofty beliefs indeed, but the political animal in the president was far from dead. His party, the Democrats, had fared badly in the mid-term elections of 1894 and he was willing to support public opinion and court voter opinion regarding the British position. The Monroe Doctrine had become the undeniable vital center of American foreign policy, a symbol of power and importance, and Cleveland was confident of its appeal in public debate. Some of his critics were ready to remind him and the nation that in April 1895, when the British temporarily occupied the Venezuelan town of Corinto he had been slow to protest. Now he wanted to exorcise the devil of inaction if not indifference by endorsing a tough stand. Finally all the talk of "war if necessary" that had flooded the newspaper columns served to take the peoples' mind off the continuing depression brought on by the Panic of '93. Yet for all of that the president may have gone too far. Would the nation follow him once the initial fury had subsided?

The answer is No. More sober judgments prevailed. Shortly after Cleveland sent his message to congress a memorial appeared in the Congressional Record. Signed by hundreds of members of parliament it called for arbitration of the Venezuelan problem as part of a larger proposal for a wide-ranging Anglo-American Arbitration Treaty. This tended to lessen agitation by American jingoes. The war scare also had a negative impact, the economy was even then struggling to get out of the doldrums. Business men in particular feared the effects of rumors of war and preferred a peaceful settlement. British investments, always a significant factor in the commercial world, began to pull out, leaving Wall Street with a bad case of the jitters. The shaky economic edifice began to look like an albatross around the neck of Cleveland and his administration. On another level of concern there was a growing belief Americans and Britons should be friends rather than enemies as many stressed a common blood line and cultural connexion with the erstwhile mother country. To make matters more uncomfortable for Cleveland

and others who seemed willing to flirt with war the chaplain of the senate prayed for peace as the tide began to run more and more strongly in favor of compromise. Perhaps Salisbury had acted more wisely than he knew.

London Is Calm. During these weeks of uncertainty in America England remained calm. Given the far flung reality of the British empire wherein there seemed always to be minor flare-ups a petty boundary disagreement in South America was not the sort of matter that justified war, or talk of war. There was a growing sentiment, in contrast, that held war between the English-speaking peoples would be a disaster too wicked to contemplate. This outlook Joseph Chamberlain spelled out in a speech in his home city of Birmingham in January 1898. "While I would look with Horror upon anything in the nature of fratricidal strife I should look forward with pleasure to the possibility of the Stars and Stripes and the Union Jack together in defense of a common cause sanctioned by humanity and justice." Similar expressions of friendship were part of the Anglo-American Arbitration Memorial. It contained, for example, the following statement. "Whatever may be the differences between the Governments in the present and in the future, all English-speaking peoples united by race, language and religion should regard war as the one absolutely intolerable mode of settling differences of the Anglo-American family." No doubt such feelings were honestly conveyed though they tended to ignore the demographic realities of America, the great melting pot. The establishment was nevertheless largely Anglo-American in makeup. The Irish had yet to infiltrate the corridors of power. Such public appeals were echoed by Arthur James Balfour, the leader of the House of Commons, giving them the imprimatur of ministry and legislature alike. (*See Document No. 3.*)

England and the Boers. Closely tied to the rising pro-American sentiment were dangerous new developments in South Africa. The raid by Leander Starr Jameson into Boer territory in December 1895, prompted an ominous-sounding note from the German Kaiser. The so-called Kruger telegram, sent to Paul Kruger, the president of the Boer Republic, congratulated the Boers on their successful challenge of British adventuring "without appealing to the help of a friendly power." In London this was interpreted that German interference would have been forthcoming had Kruger but called for it. For a fuller understanding of

Anglo–American diplomacy in 1895–1896 as well as in the years immediately ahead, the Boer War of 1899–1902, it is essential to realize how
heavily the British were committed to maintaining their presence and
their power in South Africa. It was part of their overall determination
to control the continent from Cape to Cairo. From the time the British
took control of the Cape Colony in 1815 there was tension between
them and the Dutch farmers who had settled the interior, areas later
known as the Transvaal and the Orange Free State. Federation of those
republics ruled by the Boers, as the Dutch were called, and the lands
controlled by Great Britain was an idea whose time had not come by the
1880s. Attempts by the British to accomplish it by force met with disaster at Majuba Hill in 1881. This meant quasi-independence for the
Boers. Possibly the two distinct peoples could have lived together except
for the discovery of an immensely rich gold field in the Transvaal.
Thousands of foreigners, a majority of whom were British, flooded into
the territory creating new and deeper tension. These *Uitlanders* were
badly treated by Boer authorities under local law, and this was resented
by the intruders. The Jameson Raid, aimed at taking over the Transvaal,
failed utterly. Kruger might well have looked to Germany as a possible
ally should local British leaders, especially Cecil Rhodes, continue to
resort to the threat and use of force to bring about a South Africa union.
Compared to these happenings the Anglo–American disagreement
about a jungle boundary line in South America took on the dimension
of a minor misunderstanding between fundamentally friendly nations.
This was the conviction of both Downing Street and the British public.
In other words Great Britain's difficulties in the Old World prompted
the Foreign Office to seek to resolve the New World imbroglio as quickly
and as gracefully as possible. (*See Document No. 4.*)

Arbitration, Limited Success. There were good reasons both
in Washington and London to set the diplomatic wheels in motion.
From January to June in 1896 Salisbury and Olney jockeyed for advan-
tage, with Joseph Chamberlain in cooperation with Sir William Har-
court, leader of the Liberal party in the Commons, noticeably pro-
American. The outstanding issue by this juncture was not should the
United States be involved in the affair but rather the issue of control
over the land where British subjects had lived for many years. By mid-
July the parties agreed to commence formal discussions. The fact is
Olney gave way in face of British insistence that preemptive right should

guarantee these lands remain under British jurisdiction, thus excluding the issue from the arbitration process. Sir Julian Pauncefote, Her Majesty's (HM) ambassador to Washington, strongly urged his government to start the arbitration mechanism. In November an Anglo-American agreement was initialed and arbitration was a reality. Membership on the commission was composed of jurists from each country, but the Venezuelans were to be excluded. Strong protests from Caracas led the United States to yield one of its seats, whereupon the Venezuelan government nominated Melville Fuller, chief justice of the United States. It was not until October 1899 that the tribunal rendered its verdict, which amounted to a validation of the Schomburgk line of 1840.

The one remaining diplomatic business affecting the two governments was the broader proposal for an Anglo-American Arbitration Treaty which if entered into would have virtually ruled out war between the two nations. The foreign office had given its approval and in the United States Olney, Cleveland, and the new president, William McKinley, were solidly behind it. The United States Senate, after introducing what had been termed ruinous provisions of amendment, nonetheless rejected its version of the treaty. The vote was three short of the required two-thirds majority with 43 in favor and 26 against.

Assessment. How then to assess the outcome of this first phase of the Anglo-American rapprochement that would lead on to the special relationship? There are three interrelated estimates. First, the agreement to bring about the settlement was popular in both countries, and this generated further good will. Second, the Monroe Doctrine, or the American insistence on its application to the Venezuelan boundary line settlement in what was strictly speaking an Anglo-Venezuelan affair, enhanced the prestige of the doctrine, as British influence in the region was correspondingly reduced. Finally, the outcome underscored the growing conviction that there was a natural friendship obtaining between the two English-speaking nations, accompanied by a deepening mutual regard in a world of competing alliances.

Ironically the confrontation over the boundary dispute had awakened leaders in both countries to the repugnance of war between Great Britain and the United States, and in the end promoted a strong feeling that measures, formal and informal, needed to be undertaken to assure that such a misfortune was never to come about. Viewed as a diplomatic phenomenon it seemed to be the result of drift and not mastery, at least until it became very clear cooperation was the best way to proceed. But could such a flowering of amicable diplomacy come about solely on its own, or were there deeper and more persuasive underlying considerations? In a final analysis were subcutaneous elements to make it likely for Britain and America to join hands after more than a century of separation? There were indeed numerous subsurface links based in language and literature, in law and government, in preferences and prejudices, when taken all in all, help explain how the shock and animosity of 1895 could be transformed, virtually by 1899, into an abiding and admiring respect mutually felt. A fuller understanding of the special relationship and its staying power, a span of years now amounting to a century, requires an exploration of the cultural and emotional ties that were to bind Britain and America together.

The Role of Culture. The cultural link has been identified as probably the most important connection, a strength that is admittedly difficult to render in practical terms. It existed, nonetheless, and had existed in muted form prior to the events of the 1890s. And for no other reason than a common tongue. It is by means of a common language that values, feelings of love and hate, and the aspirations of peoples are conveyed with awareness and appreciation. Throughout much of the nineteenth century this was by no means a relationship between equals. English literature was foremost and Americans could only wonder and envy it. The Hawthornes and Whitmans were there to be sure, but compared to the British their numbers were far fewer. There was a fullness and a richness of old England to draw upon whereas life in young America was raw still. London was the great city and England the mother country and together they exercised a fascination for American readers. Such was the power of a common language, irrespective of the literary form whether it be hymn or a popular novel. When William Howard Taft was courting Nellie Herron, their favorite writer was George Eliot (Mary Ann Evans) and their favorite novel was *Mill on the Floss*, which they read aloud together. In art and architecture as well there was a sympathy of styles and themes. The Georgian fashion in buildings was taken up by American builders and flourished under the name of Federal. The aesthetic sense was held in common. And much the same may be said of landscape and portrait painting. The cultural exchange has been thought of as occurring as that between the Greeks and the Romans. Just as Greece was a source of great cultural and intellectual originality which Rome was to adapt and embody in its civilization so too America drew heavily on English tastes and values, tailoring them of course to fit a New World environment. By the close of the nineteenth century this commonality had begun to express itself in the form of an increasing interest in the history and the future of the English-speaking nations. (*See Document No. 5.*)

In matters of language American English was innovative, ready to accommodate fresh vocabulary from whatever tongue whenever there was the need and opportunity to do so. Admittedly the New World setting made the introduction of new words easier than in old England. But what underscores the cultural tie is that Englishmen began to incorporate Americanisms whereas Americans seemed less comfortable when it came to use any term grounded on sharp class distinctions. For example, charwomen for those assigned menial tasks in a house never gained currency in the United States. It has been said that what the Americans were doing was inventing language much as the Elizabethans had done in their time when life was more vital or at least more novel. Suspicions and resentments so very common early in the century became much less pronounced and understanding grew apace.

The Emotional Quotient. Emotions often play a part and on occasion a decisive one in human affairs as registered at the national and international levels. And because of the historical circumstances surrounding the birth and growth of the United States, the feelings of people, and of people in government, must be treated as a feature of British-American diplomacy, 1895-1917. If the cultural links can be identified only with a careful regard for generalizations the emotional state of the two English-speaking peoples raises the need for more cautious judgments. And yet it would be no mere oversight but a mistake were emotions not taken into account. It was Viscount Castlereagh while foreign secretary who as early as 1820 observed: "there are no two states whose friendly relations are of more practical value to each other and whose hostility so inevitably and so immediately entails upon both the most mischief [than] the British and American nations." Such a judgment took on greatly added meaning once the United States entered actively into world affairs.

A New Spirit. An account of the ups and downs of the Anglo-American relationship need not be reviewed here. What must be estimated, however, and it can be only an estimate, is the state of feelings in the 1890s. Disturbances between the two countries were virtually at an end by 1871. This was due in part to their divergent postures. The neo-imperialism of Great Britain stood in sharp contrast to the isolationism of the United States. But it is also worthy to note such criticism as did occur between the nations was more certain to rest on fact and analysis rather than on a sense of past injustices and mistakes. British commentators on America and its ways, including Rudyard Kipling (whose wife was American), James Bryce, H. G. Wells and others gave accurate accounts of political corruption and that overweening desire of Americans to make money. Americans inclined to be less resentful of such castigations in part because they were true and in part because of their tendency to shrug off the judgments of outsiders. In turn Americans were largely indifferent to what went on in the Empire during the post-1870 era. Unmindfulness rarely produces anger, or love for that matter. Some pockets of anti-British sentiment could be found but this was not typical of the total body social. As for the English there was a growing willingness to concede that the United States could be the wave of the future, a wave that British might well have to ride. Correspondingly there was a willingness by Americans to take the British at their word on the premise that a reasonable accommodation of their interests was both possible and preferable. The emotional state of the Anglo-American relationship, which was not yet the special relationship, was conducive to such developments. How this would play out as the next century passed into history would, of course, depend on the men and the events, the men who were to emerge as leaders in each government and such events as would or would not make it profitable for those working in the fields of diplomacy to endure the nettles in order to grasp the rose. (*See Document No. 6.*)

CHAPTER 2

ANNUS MIRABILIS

Enter Theodore Roosevelt. To Theodore Roosevelt, who was to make an unmatched contribution to the new found friendship between Great Britain and the United States, the year 1898 was *annus mirabilis*. It signaled London's preference for an American victory in its war with Spain, a war in which TR had taken an active part both as Assistant Navy Secretary and Colonel of the Rough Riders. As he put it, Britain's solicitous attitude "worked a complete revolution in my feelings and that of the continent at that time opened my eyes to the other side." In consequence, he felt "very strongly that the English-speaking peoples are now closer together than for a century and that every effort should be made to keep them together, for their interests are fundamentally the same, and they are far more closely akin, not merely in blood, but in feeling and in principle. . . . " All this did not make Roosevelt an Anglomaniac. It was a matter simply of the dovetailing of British and American global priorities. But he was impelled to tell one of his close English friends that he fully endorsed "the view of my Lt. Parker of the Gatlings when he overhead him telling the Russian naval attaché at Santiago that 'the two branches of the Anglo-Saxon race had come together and that together we can whip the world, Prince, we can whip the world'." Such effusions of solidarity meant little enough in diplomatic circles in 1898 but by 1901, after Roosevelt succeeded to the presidency, this outlook was bound to have a decided effect on the development of Anglo-American relations.

The years 1898–1902 witnessed a turning point. In 1898 Great Britain resisted pressure from the continental powers to thwart America's war against Spain over Cuba. It did so in opposition to Queen Victoria's known sympathies for the Spanish Queen; the royal matriarch continued to be troubled whenever a king or queen had fallen on evil days. Neither British good offices nor military help of any kind would be forthcoming to spare Spain the humiliation of defeat, and the further loss of empire. In 1899 the controversy over the Venezuelan boundary dispute was finally laid to rest, to the satisfaction of both London and Washington. That same year the Boer War flared up and on the face of it Americans might be expected to favor the underdog Boers as they battled for their political independence and their cultural identity. The United States government, however, maintained a species of neutrality that worked in favor of Britain. In the colorful way he had with words Theodore Roosevelt put it this way: the Boer farmers were belated Cromwellians, but the English language must be spoken south of the Zambesi. (*See Document No. 7.*) True, new challenges to Anglo-American unity were just over the horizon. In 1901 United States policy regarding Central America, and especially the construction of an interoceanic canal, crystallized in such a way as to force Britain to yield to American presence and power. In like manner United States demands at the time of the Alaskan boundary dispute were met, at London's expense. By that year, 1903, the new understanding had proceeded so far as to become a relationship of equals. Or to put it another way, an equal partnership of the two leading English-speaking nations had been brought about. Once it was recognized for what it was international politics would never again be the same.

Cuba Libre. The Spanish-American War was, in the American view, a war to free Cuba from old style European imperialism. It was a conflict between the United States and Spain, and only between them, having nothing to do with Great Britain; just as the Venezuelan boundary affair did not directly concern the United States. These juxtapositions should be borne in mind in as much as they help to define the nature of the ongoing relationship. But unlike the United States in 1895 the London government in 1898 had no intention of allowing itself to become involved in either the build up to hostilities, in the fighting should it come to that, or in the peace settlement which was to follow. England remained an interested observer, by no means indifferent to the outcome because it saw in an American victory another sign that the United States had arrived on the world scene as a great power, and a friendly power as well.

The United States entered the war out of mixed motives, a compound that proved to be a fuel driving the will to conquer in the far Pacific as well as the nearby Caribbean. Navalism, the fruit of Captain Mahan's writings and the discipleship he gained from them, commercialism, as American business men eyed opportunities close to home and in distant China, humanitarianism, with its desire to lighten the burden of oppression from the backs of the Cuban people, and patriotism, an awakened realization by the American people that their republic had come of age—all these factors came together to ignite the warrior urge. America was poised to assume its place among the powers. Had there been no cry of *Cuba libre* it seems fair to argue that some such cause would had to have been invented because of an irresistible dynamic possessing the nation.

Remember the Maine. The sinking of the USS *Maine* in February 1898, was the point of no return. The atrocities committed against the Cuban people were horrifying and aroused the American government and people to take preventive action. It was a genuine war of liberation. The European nations judged it differently, an act of aggression against a weaker nation at its most vulnerable point, disguised as an act of kindness. But in terms of British-American diplomacy the only question was what, if anything, would Lord Salisbury's government do to promote or to retard concerted action on the part of the continental nations to spare Spain the agony of defeat and surrender? The question invites examination on two levels, public opinion which in a country like England was of no mean importance, and that of government policy. The two can not be readily separated. Public opinion clearly favored American action in Cuba. Both *The Times* and *Economist* in leader articles published within days of one another in April 1898, applauded Washington's reasons for taking a hard line with Spanish rule in Cuba. The island and its people were victims of the abuse of unlimited power. When some weeks before the DePuy de Lôme letter had come to light, London newspapers expressed dismay at the Spanish ambassador's attack on President McKinley as an "ear to the ground" politician. Telegrams deploring this insult were dispatched to Washington via the British embassy from Queen Victoria and the Lord Mayor of London. After the sinking of the *Maine* crowds had gathered in front of the American embassy to pay their respects. As the *London Chronicle* put it: "at bottom in all regards America is—to use phraseology from sport—'our side' in the great game of the world." The poet laureate, Alfred Austin, sang of Anglo-American friendship. Ambassador John Hay reported that British sympathy for America was everywhere, "beyond doubt I find it wherever I go." As significant as all this is, what was the position taken by Her Majesty's government?

Europe's Concern. In the month before war was declared, or in March 1898, support for Spain among the continental nations was so strong that the word "intervention" was talked of in the foreign ministries in Vienna, Berlin, and Paris. London remained aloof. Sir Julian Pauncefote, the British ambassador to the United States, was under strict instruction not to encourage Austrian, German or French envoys accredited to Washington to believe that Great Britain would be part of any diplomatic manoeuvre to influence American policy makers, out of respect for Anglo-American friendship. Pressure was building up, none-theless, as war appeared to be more and more likely. This was the sense of the foreign envoys. Alarmed, the ambassadors from Austria-Hungary, Germany, France, Italy, Russia, and Great Britain composed a note urg-ing moderation on the part of the McKinley administration. Paunce-fote, very much in favor of peace rather than war, allowed himself to be drawn into this circle. The president was unmoved and offered neither concessions nor promises. Pauncefote's superiors in London held that the note was more likely to hasten war than prevent it. A second note, using the French text written by Ambassador Cambon, was interpreted as more brash. The foreign office, including Salisbury, preferred caution to forcefulness but said nothing because Pauncefote had foolishly al-lowed his name to appear again among the signers. The formal British position was that it was "inexpedient" to take sides. In short, Great Brit-ain was against any form of intervention, and that gave Pauncefote the reason to go along with the need to reassure the State Department of a strict British neutrality. On the eve of the war there is little doubt the people and the statesmen of the old mother country were prepared to stand by the United States, come what may.

Britain's Support. During the course of the war, barely four months in duration, there was recurring evidence that Anglo-American friendship was on a steady course. The widespread belief given to the story about the battle of Manila during which Captain Chichester of the Royal Navy manoeuvered two ships to protect Dewey's fleet from a possible German flank attack produced both pro-British and an anti-German feeling. Myth or reality, it makes very little difference; history is often a matter of what people thought to be true rather than what the facts conveyed. As for the future of the Philippines high ranking of-ficials in London were known to encourage the Americans to take con-trol of the island group, thereby strengthening Britain's Far Eastern position at the expense of Germany. All this seems to affirm Theodore Roosevelt's account of Lt. Parker's boast that together the two English-speaking nations could whip the world.

All during the summer of 1898 crowds in London were heard cheering for the Americans, and on occasion voices were raised, singing the Star Spangled Banner in front of the United States embassy. The American flag was the only foreign standard flown at the March Past on the Salisbury Plain that summer. London newspapers were full of accounts of American gallantry. This added up to more than lip service. Before George Dewey set sail for Manila he was able to resupply ships of his squadron only with the aid of the British at Mir Bay. In late June when Admiral Camara led his Spanish fleet through the Mediterranean on its way east he put into Alexandria to take on coal, water and other needs only to have Lord Cromer, the British Agent General in Egypt, arrange to have permission denied, whereupon the Spanish fleet returned home.

As more and more stories of Britain's friendly actions were known to the American public shouts of "God save the Queen" could be daily heard. Victoria's seventy-ninth birthday was celebrated with great gusto by many newly converted Anglophiles. Over one thousand prominent Americans, a veritable who's who, signed an Address proposing friendship and support for the British Empire, something unthinkable but a few years before. American expansion was to go hand in hand with Britain on the path to world domination. Even Carl Schurz, as good a German-American as could be found, wrote approvingly of "the demonstrated display of British sympathy for the United States." In New York theaters the Stars and Stripes and the Union Jack were intertwined. 1898 truly was *annus mirabilis.*

Historical Viewpoint. The foregoing examples of Anglo-American togetherness, emotional in their response to the affairs of the moment, may be better appreciated by examining exchanges of ideas (and emotions) between important Englishmen of the era in letters to and from Theodore Roosevelt. As has been indicated TR would become the moving force in determining a workable arrangement between Washington and London as the new century unfolded. How these men thought about the rapprochement and how their thinking was influenced by a wide ranging correspondence, along with frequent personal meetings, can tell us much that explains how and why diplomacy between the White House and Whitehall was so successfully conducted.

In his formative years, when writing what was a magnum opus, *The Winning of the West*, Roosevelt insisted "during the last three centuries the spread of the English-speaking peoples over the world's waste spaces has been the most striking feature in the world's history, but also the event of all others most far-reaching in its effects and its importance." For TR this was the starting point, not only his major premise for an appraisal of modern history but a guide line for conducting contemporary diplomacy. Take, for example, his exchange of ideas with James Bryce, author of *The American Commonwealth*, written as a piece of Anglo-American history. He did so, it should be noted, with help from a number of American savants, Albert Shaw, Henry Charles Lea, Seth Low, and Theodore Roosevelt among them. The common value they shared was a faith in successful self-government as achieved by the most advanced and gifted peoples, those who spoke English. Another Roosevelt correspondent, St. Loe Strachey, editor of the *Spectator*, told TR it was all a matter of the Whig temperament and spirit, and Roosevelt agreed with him exactly: "liberty can and does reside only in moderation and an avoidance of violence and fanaticism." The two found a common hero in Thomas Macauley who "really loved liberty and hated cruelty and oppression, but was always a good party man." Roosevelt readily identified the Whig temperament and spirit with the kind of Republican party of which he wanted first to be a member and then to lead.

TR and His Friends. When it came to world affairs Roosevelt's outlook often reveals the influence of his long time friendship with Cecil Spring Rice, a British diplomat who became HM ambassador to Washington from 1913 to 1918. Spring Rice was especially wary of the new imperial Germany, and often said as much to his American friend. As early as 1897 he could be found telling TR that both England and America had reason to worry about the danger posed by the new Germany. A build up of its navy would not only threaten the British possessions east of Suez but it might also seek to defy the Monroe Doctrine. To which the future president replied: "If I were an Englishman I would seize the first opportunity to crush the German Navy." What he left unsaid was such a move would eliminate the German threat to the Americas, a danger he took fairly seriously. Spring Rice was constant and consistent in expressing his distrust of Germany, not alone because of potential trouble regarding England and America but because it was not a liberal self-governing nation. Roosevelt vowed when president that should the Germans make any misstep in the western hemisphere he would give them fair warning to get out before going into action. Such a policy fitted nicely with Great Britain's grand strategy.

TR prided himself on being an historian, and often exhibited the historian's view of the past. The English historian, G. O. Trevelyan (the first British professional to take the side of the colonists in the War of the American Revolution) was also a champion of the Whig interpretation of history. By this he understood that in certain nations progress was being made because people were ruling themselves. Conversely, nations ruled by kaisers or czars were unrestrained by elected legislatures or written constitutions. The world could trust the former while having deep seated suspicions about the latter. Another English contact, Arthur Hamilton Lee, when he sat in the House of Commons was denominated "Member for America," so pronounced was he when it came to supporting America and all things American. To Lee "the future relations between England and America are going to form the joint upon which the whole future of the Anglo-Saxon race will hinge." Such an assertion has only to be linked to the opening passages in *The Winning of the West* to appreciate the oneness of mind and spirit which would be a working supposition once Roosevelt was in the White House.

A Natural Identity. The natural identity with the principle and practice of self-government rendered United States policy toward the Boer War somewhat awkward, first for the McKinley administration and then for Roosevelt himself. Adding to the uneasiness was British determination to use superior force to form a union of South African states and territories that would include, by necessity, the Transvaal and the Orange Free State. Within Britain itself, in fact, there were many naysayers when brute conquest was called for. Among them was Spring Rice. As he told Roosevelt, "if I were not an Englishman I should certainly sympathize with the Boers—and we can't possibly object if other people do it." The official American attitude of both McKinley and Roosevelt was neutrality, nonetheless, and in effect it made the United States government to appear pro-British. This can be explained largely in terms of a desire to remain on good terms with a nation which, while it might make mistakes, was still America's best friend.

But what of the diplomacy undergirding British-American relations relative to the Boer War? In general the continental powers were hostile to the war England was waging. Countries such as Germany or France had peculiarly nationalistic motives for opposing the expansion of the Empire. Under such circumstances United States neutrality appeared positively benign and was so interpreted by London. Within the McKinley administration Secretary of State Hay was completely given over to the British cause and was utterly determined to make no move that suggested hostility to England. William McKinley's refusal to give any commitment to a plan to produce a negotiated settlement when he was visited by a Boer delegation surely reflected Hay's thinking. Acting in concert with the United States Germany and France might well have brought London to arbitration; lacking American cooperation such prospects had too little foundation. In that same year, 1900, there was a certain amount of agitation in the United States, championing the Boer cause, particularly when the presidential campaign was underway. American soldiers fighting a bushwhacking war against the Filipino insurrectionaries and justifying the need to take such measures had much to do with neutralizing the Boer issue. Influential voices in the Senate, including those of Henry Cabot Lodge and Cushman Davis, chairman of the Senate Foreign Relations Committee, were outspokenly pro-British. Their argument, namely, because London in 1898 had acted in ways favorable to the United States could the United States do less in 1899 for the British, may have been an oversimplification but it had a powerful appeal.

To sum up, British avoidance of defeat in South Africa, which would have gravely weakened its power and prestige vis-à-vis the major powers, fit in with America's "large policy." Washington both wanted and needed a strong British Empire in order to firm up its own world position. It should be understood, nevertheless, each of the two English-speaking nations intended to pursue its own agenda. Witness: the Anglo-Japanese Treaty of 1902 and the insistence by President Roosevelt, however well disposed he and his administration might be toward Great Britain, that an American built and paid for canal must be fortified by the United States as an extension of its sovereign territory.

CHAPTER 3

TIME OF TESTING

Areas of Concern. The de facto understanding obtaining between London and Washington, however promising, had yet to meet and surmount a real challenge to its durability. Then and only then would it be realistic to speak of a "great rapprochement." The time of testing was at hand. It began when it was clear the United States intended to construct and fortify a canal across the waist of the Americas, perhaps in Nicaragua, perhaps at Panama. This time of trial would also include a dispute over the boundary of Alaska where it abutted Canadian territory. Thrown in for good measure was the matter of Venezuelan debt collection in which both Great Britain and Germany figured. Should these several obstacles be cleared then a secured understanding of Anglo-American diplomatic cooperation for years to come would be in place. What is especially noteworthy is that in each of the foregoing affairs the United States would have the initiative which meant that Great Britain had been reduced in status to that of a reactive partner. To some extent this was due to the zeal of Theodore Roosevelt once he was president. Yet he was himself only playing the cards placed in his hands by events of the years after 1895. When President McKinley in his 1898 message to Congress called for "some definite action" aimed at getting a canal project underway it demonstrated that events, and more specifically the Spanish-American War—were forcing the issue. Admittedly, TR would take more vigorous steps but not even the dynamic Teddy could have made the dirt fly in Panama if the overall circumstances had not worked to ripen the fruit about to fall into the American basket.

The diplomacy involved in clearing the way to canal construction was intertwined with the settlement of a boundary line disagreement in Alaska Territory between Canada and the United States. In as much as treaties were involved both in the Central American issue and that of the Pacific Northwest the art and the management of diplomacy became the keys to maintaining Anglo-American relations on even keel. Before a detailed discussion of the diplomatic give-and-take is pursued it may be useful to review the issues in broader historical outline.

In 1850 London and Washington signed the Clayton-Bulwer Treaty. It came about in a curious way when in 1848 Nicaragua granted the United States exclusive right of way across its territory should building of a canal become feasible. But President Taylor did not send the draft treaty to the Senate for consideration. Secretary of State John Clayton, anxious to reassure the British as to American intentions, initiated discussions with the British minister to Washington, Sir Henry Lytton Bulwer. A treaty with the following stipulations was approved by the Senate; the vote was 42 to 10. The terms included: 1) agreement never to obtain or exercise exclusive control over an isthmian ship canal, or to fortify it; 2) a guarantee of the neutrality and security of the canal; 3) agreement to keep any future canal open to British and American nationals on terms of equality; 4) and a pledge not to colonize, occupy, or exercise dominion over any part of Central America. (*See Document No. 8.*)

Changed Circumstances. What appeared as a reasonable arrangement in 1850 had become a challenge to American supremacy in the Western Hemisphere in general and to the Caribbean basin in particular in the wake of the Spanish-American War. Add the fact that there was after 1898 a new American presence in the mid and far Pacific, the need to make it possible for the United States navy to man battle stations in both oceans became more imperative still. The canal therefore was a must for American planners, commercially no less than militarily. Had the Clayton-Bulwer Treaty been the only issue on the table in the period 1899–1901 it is possible, though not certain, that London would have graciously conceded to the expectations the Washington government entertained about an inter-oceanic waterway. Put another way, the problem of establishing a boundary line that would satisfy contending American and Canadian claims over the complex chain of islands off the common coast line appeared to stand athwart such an agreement. From the time the United States had purchased Alaska from Russia in 1867 the line of demarcation between British Columbia and American Alaska had remained ill defined. The maps theretofore used by the British and the Russians dating from 1825 were so vague that both London and Washington were able to make extravagant claims to the disputed islands. Until gold was discovered in the Yukon in 1896–97 the issue lay dormant. This discovery led not only to a gold rush, but a rush to judgment respecting the boundary line. 1898 saw the signing of a protocol which set up a Joint High Commission. Its purpose was to resolve the rival claims although other matters, including the use of alien labor, mining rights, and fur seals, were also to be taken up. The creation of the Joint High Commission amounted to no more than a holding action however as each side sparred for advantage. In his annual message to Congress in December McKinley sounded a conciliatory note because he recognized the likelihood that British negotiators would be seeking a quid pro quo: in return for concessions to American determination to build an isthmian canal Washington would be expected to yield on the boundary issue. The fact is that as of December 1898 the State Department was preparing to ask Britain to make fundamental changes to the terms of the Clayton-Bulwer Treaty. The question which emerged was this: could the canal issue and the boundary issue be solved, not piecemeal but as a result of a master stroke of British-American diplomacy? This indeed constituted a time of testing the resolve on the part of the leaders of both countries to lay deep the foundations of Anglo-American friendship, based not on sentiment but on the distinct yet mutually beneficial vital interests of each nation.

Negotiations Begin. Negotiations aimed at clearing the diplomatic underbrush that had accumulated since 1850, thus making way for British acceptance of an American built and fortified canal, fall into three discernible segments. The first of these is marked by McKinley's December, 1898, message to Congress and the rejection of new American demands by the Foreign Office in February 1899, insisting that the Clayton-Bulwer Treaty remain in force. The second phase begins in January, 1900 when Secretary Hay revives negotiations which by the end of the next month saw the completion of a draft of a new convention. It was not until December, 1900, and Hay's submission of an amended convention, phase three, that things began to move perceptibly forward, concluding with the Senate's approval of the Second Hay-Pauncefote Treaty in December 1901.

It is well to bear in mind that William McKinley was an imperialist president, and therefore not surprisingly he told the Congress of the pressing need to construct an isthmian canal. The language he chose to use left no doubt of his determination to see the job done. A canal "was more than ever indispensable to that intimate and ready interconnection between our eastern and western seaboards demanded by the annexation of the Hawaiian Islands and the prospective expansion of our influence and commerce in the Pacific . . . our national policy now more than ever calls for its control by this Government." McKinley concluded by saying he expected Congress would "duly appreciate and wisely act upon" his proposal for an American canal. Coming as it did as part of an official American state paper alarm bells went off in London and prompted Sir Julian Pauncefote, HM ambassador to Washington to inquire more particularly regarding the president's announcement. What exactly did the administration have in mind? (*See Document No. 9.*)

According to Secretary John Hay who was to field Pauncefote's inquiry, the president was merely verbalizing what the nation was hoping for, and a recognition Congress would have to vote the funds for construction once Senate approval had been given regarding treaty obligations. Beyond that Hay proposed to Sir Julian that he seek his government's agreement to commence talks to consider modification, in detail but not in principle, of the Clayton–Bulwer Treaty. The secretary of state, who certainly deserves to be recognized as the prime mover in this undertaking, instructed Henry White, the American chargé d'affaires in London, to sound out the Foreign Office along the same lines. Things appear to have gone smoothly for White; on December 21, 1898, Pauncefote was told he had considerable discretion in further talks with Hay. The two statesmen closely involved in such discussions were on the best personal terms. Yet there was no agreement between them with it came to a draft of a treaty for almost a year. As Pauncefote advised the Foreign Office in December 1899, "the treaty was prepared by Mr. Hay, but on the model of a draft supplied to him by me at his request." Obviously their cooperation, if not collaboration, was telling.

Draft Treaty. What, then, were the terms of the draft treaty? In effect, the Clayton-Bulwer Treaty was to be amended rather than replaced, and the general principle of a neutral canal, neutralization, remained intact. The most important amendment to the old treaty, termed the Davis amendment, offered by Cushman Davis, was that construction of a canal was conceded to the United States with full rights for its regulation and management. There was a further definition of the rules on neutralization, something that would prove a stumbling block for acceptance by the Senate. Not only was the canal to remain open and free to all nations in time of war as in time of peace but the canal was not subject to the rules of blockade, and no fortification could be constructed for its defense. All the United States could do was to "police" the canal.

Britain Hesitates. During the year 1899 as the Hay-Pauncefote talks proceeded Lord Salisbury sought advice from a variety of professionals. Sir John Ardagh, head of military intelligence, argued that having the United States in full control of the canal was a bad idea while the Lords of Admiralty concluded that such a situation could have a negative impact on the supremacy enjoyed by the Royal Navy. The Board of Trade was alone in being well disposed to the "general" proposition of an American owned canal. Basic to any concessions Great Britain might make was the widely held view that the United States must give way to Canada when the boundary was at last determined. It had become clear that the Joint High Commission was unlikely to be able to produce the long awaited settlement. Pauncefote was informed as early as February that acceptance of the draft convention would also have to be tied to United States concessions regarding trade with Cuba, Puerto Rico and the Philippine Islands. What was being envisioned in London was an overall agreement, worldwide in dimension, with all outstanding issues resolved in a grand master stroke. (*See Document No. 10.*)

One might be justified in concluding that it was a complex set of circumstances prompting the Foreign Office to move as it did. The fact is that some progress had been made by the Joint High Commission, enough perhaps to persuade the cabinet that more progress could be made, given enough time. A second consideration was the state of American public and political opinion. The Americans were chaffing at the bit, increasingly impatient with British foot dragging and suspicious of the ultimate designs of "perfidious Albion." Finally there was the lack of success in the Boer War. The winter of 1899–1900 saw the British army mired in what appeared to many observers as a no-win situation. The continental powers were restless and perhaps preparing to interfere in the name of a negotiated peace; Russia might well take advantage of British distress in South Africa to challenge the Empire in Asia. All the foregoing are, of course, general considerations which strategic planners in Whitehall had to take under advisement. More specifically on January 21, 1900 Pauncefote informed the Foreign Office that unless the draft treaty were approved Congress might vote to abrogate the Clayton-Bulwer Treaty thereby ending the deadlock and creating a volatile set of circumstances. Such was the thinking of John Hay. It was left to Joseph Chamberlain, the Colonial Secretary, to appeal to the Canadians to put empire before dominion. Apparently he had struck just the right note because Canada, almost without hesitation, agreed to defer. Whereupon Pauncefote was instructed to sign the draft treaty which he did on February 2, 1900. The next step was the Senate.

Senate Rejects. To the surprise of few and to the bitter disappointment of Secretary Hay the Senate rejected the treaty except for amendments which it proposed to insert. President McKinley refused to accept the resignation of John Hay as secretary of state as an act of frustration but not of despair and Hay remained in office. The Senate amendments, if finally incorporated in a signed treaty, would have changed the document drastically. In the article dealing with neutralization and nonfortification the Senate insisted that none of the restrictions on United States power and authority contained in the article "shall apply to measures which the United States may find it necessary to take for securing its own forces, the defence of the United States and the maintenance of public order." The best that Hay could hope for at this stage was to persuade the British government to extend the ratification time table by several months, which was agreed to. Yet the treaty came under further pressure for concessions by Britain when the Senate Committee of Foreign Relations made more stipulations. One of these called for the new treaty to supersede the Clayton-Bulwer convention and another that the article inviting other nations to sign the treaty and thereby agree to abide by it should be scrapped. President McKinley was known to be prepared to go along with the Senate in all particulars, unwilling to risk popular displeasure. Pauncefote urged the cabinet to accept the Senate version, lest the result be a unilateral abrogation of Clayton-Bulwer. But if the end of this diplomatic chess game was in sight, there were still moves to be made by each side.

New Man, New Style. By this time Lord Lansdowne had assumed the portfolio of Foreign Secretary. His style proved to be more dynamic than that of the cautious Salisbury. Lansdowne was determined to salvage what he could in protecting British interests. His tactic was to reject the treaty as a ploy while he endeavored to get better terms. And he deliberately chose not to announce this until Congress had adjourned in mid-March 1901. This rejection hinged on certain interests vital to Britain but of no great consequence to the United States.

One example was the provision that there be only two signatories to the agreement, whereas the British preferred that all parties whose interests might be involved, as was the case with Germany or France, should also be invited to recognize the fact of American domination in the area. Lansdowne accepted that United States power and presence should be the determinating factor in any future naval actions in the Caribbean. While Lansdowne delayed, Hay proceeded to write an alternate draft, which was handed to Sir Julian in late April 1901. This new draft dropped the wording of the Davis amendment, no mention was made of fortification, the Clayton-Bulwer convention was to be superseded, but other powers were not invited to enter upon the protocol. This last consideration met serious resistance in London. Lansdowne however preferred only to insist that all nations should be invited to accept the terms of the treaty in so far as they might be affected by them. The treaty was signed November 18, 1901 and within a month and upon the strong recommendation of the Foreign Relations Committee the full Senate by a vote of 72 to 6 gave approval. Among other results this second Hay-Pauncefote Treaty signaled British acceptance that, to recall Olney boast of some years before, the United States was indeed sovereign in the Western Hemisphere. (*See Document No. 11.*)

Canal Fortification. Theodore Roosevelt as president may add further insight to the feeling of good will and cooperation in the diplomatic revolution which was now in full progress. From the outset of the canal discussions, even as governor of New York, Roosevelt had insisted that any interoceanic waterway had to be American built, American paid for, and American fortified. These views were well known because he had avowed them openly and frequently. The very day the Senate voted for the treaty, December 17, one of TR's closest English friends, Arthur Hamilton Lee, wrote him of his delight that opposition to the treaty had faded. Because of the ever strengthening spirit of Anglo-American friendship Lee told the president that in his view it was time for his government formally to recognize the Monroe Doctrine because it would warn "foreigners" of the "large measure of common understanding between the two great sections of the English-speaking people." Roosevelt replied, less effusively, "I must say how pleased I am by the ratification of the treaty. Really, I think it is as much in your interest as in ours." The mood engendered by the signing of the Hay-Pauncefote Treaty, as it turned out, would facilitate settlement of the Alaska boundary line, in the political and diplomatic processes of which Theodore Roosevelt played nothing less than a dominating part. An examination of the details of settlement can lead to no other conclusion.

Alaska and All That. In the context of the times a settlement of the Alaska boundary line was as pressing an issue as that involved in the canal diplomacy. It may appear otherwise at a distance of a century but such was the irritation and distrust registered by Canadians and Americans alike that the three thousand miles of unfortified frontier might itself be unsustained. It was a complex matter that clamored for attention, the demarcation of the boundary line a *sine qua non* of stable Anglo–American relations. Considered in its particulars it was a dispute over a few islands of limited importance and thousands of square miles of very inviting real estate. But such a view is misleading as an examination of the depth of feelings on both sides amply demonstrates.

Alaska was a frontier and in the history of frontiers in North America they can be unruly areas, liable to rash actions and capable of enflaming passions hard to contain. In 1901 rumors spread that the British were about to seize Skagaway, snatching it out from under the nose of the Americans. At the same time other rumors circulated that Canadian Yukon territory was to be taken away from Canada by American miners, acting on the established practice that a claim supported by the larger number of settlers would and should win out. Happily cooler heads prevailed in Washington and in Ottawa. Nonetheless, lurking in the back of people's minds was the thought that gold or deposits of other valuable metals could be discovered almost any place, a feeling keeping tensions high. McKinley and later on Roosevelt were both petitioned by American miner groups to take the action necessary to protect their interests. Once in the White House Roosevelt would become increasingly adamant about the validity of American claims, to the consternation of the Ottawa government.

Extraneous conditions fortunately worked to distract from any sense of urgency about a boundary settlement. The Boer War continued to drag on, leaving London with little desire to become embroiled with the United States. Lord Salisbury's declining health also militated against an active Foreign Office move and the death of Sir Julian Pauncefote weakened the British position in Washington. For that matter 1902 saw Theodore Roosevelt still settling into the presidential office and its myriad responsibilities. Although he indicated to Secretary Hay that he did not like the way things had gone to date he was prepared to allow developments to proceed before he determined a fixed policy. In this latter regard Roosevelt appreciated to a remarkable degree the difficulties the British continued to face in South Africa and for that reason alone was disinclined to add to their problems by forcing the Alaska issue.

Canada Takes a Hit. A change in the diplomatic climate occurred with the resignation of Lord Salisbury as prime minister, to be replaced by Arthur James Balfour and the appointment of Sir Michael Herbert as ambassador to Washington. Both men felt the need to dispose of the ongoing boundary matter early on. Again it was a matter of the right man in the right office at the right time. The man involved was Sir Wilfred Laurier. He had come to London to attend a conference of colonial prime ministers and it was at that time Lord Lansdowne suggested to Sir Wilfred that Canada ought to be prepared to make concessions to American expectations about the boundary demarcation. Lansdowne had also informed the United States ambassador, Joseph Choate, that he deemed a restart of negotiations was in order. As he was without instructions from Washington, Choate cabled the president for advice, and was authorized to commence talks at once. At the same time TR informed Choate that in his judgment the Canadians did not have a leg to stand on, and therefore there should be no compromise. After consulting with him Lansdowne persuaded Laurier to make two concessions to the Americans: one, that Skagaway would be within American jurisdiction, and second, a board of arbitration would be organized along the lines demanded by the United States. This placed Laurier in a difficult position with his colleagues in the Canadian cabinet. Canada had always opted for an arbitration tribunal composed of an uneven number of members, whereas the United States wanted an even number, so that if there were a tie, always considered a likelihood, Washington could dismiss the ruling as inconclusive. In which case the United States would presume it was free to act as it chose to. To put it plainly, Laurier caved in to American demands. When he informed his cabinet upon returning to Ottawa his about-face was bitterly resented but given his poor health the anticompromise Canadians did not want disruption of the government in power lest that bring on new elections. What Laurier had done can be interpreted, however, as a matter of *real politik*. By 1903 the bargaining chip, stalemate over the canal, had disappeared.

Then there was the fear that spontaneous actions on the frontier border could produce a military response with unpredictable results.

To make matters worse for Laurier (and the Canadians who wanted to stand their ground against the United States in the matter of Alaska) the troubling issue of the Newfoundland fishing business surfaced once again. Laurier wanted badly to change the status of Newfoundland from that of colony to dominion, federation with Canada. That would be a good thing in itself and it would halt the drift of Newfoundland in the direction of the United States. In 1890 the Blaine–Bond convention was negotiated whereby fish imported from Newfoundland to the United States paid a low duty. London had blocked its enforcement but now Sir Richard Bond, the prime minister of Newfoundland, wanted the treaty to go into effect. If it did the inhabitants of Newfoundland figured to benefit from increased incomes. But Laurier was totally against it, fearing loss of his country's access to Atlantic as well as Pacific trade, should he yield regarding Alaska. Cornered as he seemed to be, Laurier decided he had a better chance of integrating Newfoundland than in salvaging Ottawa's claims in Alaska. His decision in no way altered the concessions already made to Ambassador Choate in London, especially regarding the composition of the arbitration tribunal.

The outlook appeared bleak for Laurier's manoeuver when the Colonial Office allowed Sir Richard Bond permission to negotiate with the United States once more. Bond came personally to Washington to promote the agreement. But at this juncture American domestic politics spoiled his efforts. New England fishermen looked upon any deal with Newfoundland to gain entry into the United States market under any concession as amounting to dumping. Senator Henry Cabot Lodge of Massachusetts worked hard and as it turned out successfully as the reciprocity treaty was defeated in the Senate. This turn of events did appear to improve Laurier's plan for integrating Newfoundland as a dominion member. (*See Document No. 12.*)

Roosevelt Forces the Issue. President Roosevelt emerged as the dominant force in bringing about a boundary settlement largely favorable to the United States. He announced he was not prepared to yield on any of the issues involved, and at least he acted as though he meant it. Further he declared that he looked upon any determination by an arbitration tribunal as entitled to no more than a "reasonable opinion" and therefore not necessarily binding. Whatever the case, the commission must be composed of an even number of members representing each side. What was his thinking in insisting on such a composition? Should there be a tie vote, which any betting man might expect to happen, the president could (and very probably would have) dismiss the proceedings as a failure whereupon the United States might take over all the disputed lands, channels, and harbors.

A draft treaty was drawn up which stipulated that all questions would be resolved by a vote of "six impartial jurists of repute" who would consider the questions submitted to them, three appointees from each side; a majority of four to decide." The expectation was, at least in Canada, that three justices of the United States Supreme Court would be chosen, the lord chancellor of Great Britain, and two Canadian men of the law who were of good repute. At this point the conflict between the United States and Britain over the Venezuelan debt problem had intensified to such a degree as to threaten Anglo-American accord, and this must be factored into the diplomatic equation. Still the Canadians delayed, suggesting that it might be wiser to place the case before the Hague Tribunal. But Theodore Roosevelt had his mind made up and was not to be dissuaded or derailed. Finally the Canadians accepted the even number members commission, but with misgivings that were to be prophetic. The Hay-Herbert Treaty was signed in Washington January 23, 1903. Senate approval followed quickly, due largely to the exertions of Henry Cabot Lodge combined with the willingness of his friend in the White House to divulge to him privately the names of the men whom he intended to nominate, one of whom was to be Lodge himself. Using a smooth bit of parliamentary procedure the senator from Massachusetts arranged that the vote be taken by voice rather than ballot, a clear indication he was unsure that it would otherwise pass.

Only in mid-February was Ambassador Herbert informed of the names of the three "jurists" the president had chosen to represent the American position: Elihu Root, George Turner, and Henry Cabot Lodge. The claims of any one of these public/political figures to eminence as a jurist were dubious. Root did possess a judicial turn of mind which he displayed in legal practice and public service, but he had never been a judge, always an advocate. George Turner, a state of Washington senator, had already expressed himself as a strong supporter of United States claims. As for Lodge, the president's closest friend and trusted adviser, he was anathema to the Canadians (and to many Americans as well). Lodge was a man who played the game ruthlessly if always within the letter of the law. Perhaps because Supreme Court justices he sounded out were unwilling to serve on the tribunal Roosevelt appears to have swung perversely in the polar opposite direction in making his appointments. Undoubtedly his choices did speak his own mind: no compromise. Just at the moment London heard the news about the commission members British–American diplomatic relations were being tested by issues which had developed out of the financial crisis in Venezuela. If the Foreign Office was chagrined, the Canadians were insulted to the point of outrage. The Foreign Secretary nonetheless remained unmoved by Ottawa's reaction, and without waiting for a formal Canadian reply proceeded to sign the Hay–Herbert Treaty, March 3, 1903. In a much used but accurate phrase Canadian interests had been sacrificed on the altar of Anglo–American friendship.

Rather than responding to the American provocation by naming three Canadians strongly disposed to support their country's position London proposed to name three men whose reputations upheld the spirit as well as the letter of the treaty. The most eminent was Lord Alverstone, the Lord Chancellor, who was presumably to look after the interests of the empire, and two Canadians: Sir Louis A. Jette, formerly a member of the supreme court of Quebec and A. B. Alyesworth, who had been nominated to the Supreme Court of Canada, but had declined to serve for personal reasons. Because of the complexities of the issues a request was made by Canada for more time to prepare its case than the treaty had stipulated. Once again American vanity surfaced as both Lodge and Root insisted that the tribunal meet and render a judgment as prescribed. And once again the American demands prevailed. No one talked tougher than Theodore Roosevelt in holding London and Ottawa must toe the line. It was Big Stick diplomacy at its most audacious. Before and during the tribunal proceedings Roosevelt went so far as to outline his views on just how the agreement when concluded should read.

An Arbitration Decision. The tribunal commenced hearing arguments on September 3, exactly six months to the day the treaty had been signed. The issues were treated as questions and were highly specific as to boundary lines drawn, determination of ownership of islands and channels, distances of land–claims from the sea in terms of miles, the division of mountainous territory, and like detail. The fact is the Americans and Canadians were so clearly lined up against one another that the Lord Chancellor came to be the determiner of specifics and thus the architect of the final outline. The commission did not carry on its deliberations in camera. Outside pressure came from Roosevelt, who very probably was reflecting public and congressional opinion, and late in the day from Secretary Hay on the United States side. For the British prime minister Balfour hammered the point that a final determination could not be postponed. The veiled threat behind the American insistence was that in light of a failed commission ruling, the United States would take over all land and waterways, by force if need be. This was the way Balfour judged the situation and therefore expected Lord Alverstone to vote with the United States delegation to bring about the required four to two vote. The results amounted to an American victory as decisive as the Canadian defeat and were announced October 20, 1903. In the aftermath Roosevelt wrote to his close English friend, Spring Rice, there had been "literally no Canadian case at all on the main points," so that Lord Alverstone had not been pro-American in his voting but had acted instead in good faith. He concluded his letter: "It has been a very fortunate and happy thing to get the question definitely settled and out of the way," a chaste verdict not altogether consistent with the facts.

Venezuela Again. Some reference to British-American diplomacy about the Venezuelan debt crisis, the climax of which came in 1903, has already been made. Compared to the canal diplomacy or to the Alaska boundary issue it was a minor affair. But its timing had some effect on relations between London and Washington, and, it should be added, the potential for serious difficulty was certainly present. Great Britain and Germany had agreed to insist on debt repayment by Venezuela and by resort to the use of force if necessary. In other words the actions of these two Old World powers could be interpreted in the United States as a challenge to if not a violation of the Monroe Doctrine, something that could not go unanswered.

Oddly enough the words of Theodore Roosevelt, spoken before and after his elevation to the presidency were taken as indicators the United States would not object to a joint Anglo-German undertaking because their reasons for moving against the South American country were readily justified. In July 1901, Roosevelt wrote his good friend, the German diplomat Baron Speck von Sternburg: "If any South American country misbehaves toward any European country, let the European country spank it." More to the point, in Roosevelt's first annual message to Congress, December 1901, he announced: "We do not guarantee any [Latin-American] states against punishment if it misconducts itself, provided that punishment does not take the form of the acquisition of territory by any non-American power." The British and the Germans were quick to pick up on this policy statement, especially when Secretary of State Hay repeated the United States position to their official representatives in Washington. Due note was made of it in the House of Commons and in the minutes of the Kaiser's cabinet in Berlin. (*See Document No. 13.*)

Monroe Doctrine Tested Again. Within the year, or in December 1902, the two European creditor nations delivered an ultimatum to Cipriano Castro, president of Venezuela, a virtual dictator. Castro proved to be no pushover. He had come to power by the use of force in 1899, and was astute enough to see that should overt movements against him come to pass he could appeal to the United States by invoking, piously no doubt, the principles of the Monroe Doctrine. And there was a further complication touching on Anglo-American relations. With England and Germany now appearing to work together, in the American mind the former suffered a loss of face by being associated with the latter. Nor was this uneasiness confined to the United States. Strong reservations of this tandem arrangement were voiced in the British press and in the parliament. The Kruger telegram remained fresh in the minds of many in Britain and backbenchers in the Commons spoke ominously of the German threat to the supremacy of the Royal Navy. For their part Americans worried about possible German intrusion somewhere in the western hemisphere should Germany go colony hunting in what was considered a United States protected part of the world. Put plainly the Germans did not enjoy a positive image in either of the great English-speaking countries, and nothing seemed to be able to change that. It is true that from the start of their discussions as to what to do about the collection of the Venezuelan debt both countries disavowed any intention of taking, much less holding, territory. But knowledge of this only allayed and did not dismiss suspicions. At the same time Britain and Germany agreed solemnly to act in concert, an "ironclad bargain," irrespective of the repercussions that might follow their actions. From the American viewpoint the British horse was encumbered by a German cart, and could not free itself.

Castro rejected the December ultimatum. What followed was the sinking and seizing of Venezuelan gunboats, harbors were blockaded, one port bombed and another occupied by British troops. If this amounted to nothing more than a police action in the thinking of London and Berlin it soon appeared otherwise in Washington. Was all this, when taken together, not a violation of the Monroe Doctrine, or at what point in the uncertain future turn of events would it reach that stage? The opposition Liberal party pressed its attack on the Foreign Office handling of the affair especially in light of American sensitivity over the Monroe Doctrine. Had not Lansdowne allowed himself to be used by Germany, enticing him because Berlin was aware that any unilateral act would have produced a stern rebuke? Had not Britain been made to act as a shield for German ambitions in Latin America? Extreme charges to be sure but ones with an emotional appeal. And few things stir the popular emotions more than military action such as occurred after Castro's rejection of the ultimatum. In all likelihood Roosevelt did not threaten Germany with war. Sentiment mounted in the United States nonetheless, paralleled by rising concerns in Britain that plans had gone dangerously awry. Sir Michael Herbert was especially fervent in advising his government of growing American anger with events as they had developed, and he was seconded by the chargé d'affaires at the United States embassy, Henry White one of the most influential Americans living in London at the time. (*See Document No. 14.*)

Cool Heads Prevail. When Venezuela proposed arbitration a way out of the impasse was at hand. Britain and Germany quickly agreed, the latter without any special prodding from Theodore Roosevelt. Though London preferred that Roosevelt chair the arbitration proceedings the president declined if for no other reason that there were American claims against Venezuela which had to be arbitrated. Once arbitration began trouble immediately developed. The sticking point centered on which countries should be first to receive compensation. London and Berlin naturally enough expected to be paid up front, but other creditors protested. Meanwhile there was more battle action when the German ship *Panther* attacked the port of San Carlos, destroying much of its ancient works. Theodore Roosevelt well asked the question: "Are the Germans crazy?" All parties appeared to appreciate that a quick conclusion was vital if descent into war was to be avoided. In February it was agreed to refer matters to the Hague Tribunal after protocols were signed providing for early cash payments and other claims to be decided by mixed commissions.

In spite of a near flash point having been reached United States insistence upon the integrity of the Monroe Doctrine prevailed, over the misalliance of the British and Germans. The Venezuela affair had not ruptured Anglo-American friendship; if it had any effect it may have been to strengthen ties between the two powers as the ministrations of Roosevelt, Hay, and White among the Americans and Lansdowne, Herbert, Joseph Chamberlain, and Balfour in England showed that sets of leaders from each country could work together because they understood and trusted one another. Nineteen hundred one to nineteen three had been perilous years, not to be endured again for another decade when the Great War was to put heavy strains on relations between the two governments and the two peoples.

CHAPTER 4

RELATIONSHIP CONFIRMED

Sino-Japanese Connection. The complexity of British-American diplomacy, 1895–1917, can be more fully appreciated by taking up the Far Eastern policies of the two nations. Virtually nonexistent when the Venezuelan boundary issue was exercising minds and tempers, after 1898 the situation in Asia became one of the foremost considerations of policy makers in both London and Washington. And it would remain so for the next decade, a period roughly marked by the presidency of Theodore Roosevelt. This Far Eastern question expressed itself in two major ways. The future of China was one. Would China continue only as a geographic expression or would it become a geopolitical nightmare? Folded in to this larger issue was "the China trade." Every major industrial power sought to have a piece of that action and, save for the United States, had established spheres of influence in China. To say the least, the future of China was uncertain as the new century dawned. Another way of viewing the Far East might well be termed "the problem of Asia" as indeed A. T. Mahan had done in his study, thus titled, published in 1901. As judged by the Foreign Office and the State Department balance of power in that part of a changing world was an increasing preoccupation as neo-imperialism was working its way to a climax. Its culmination was to be the Great War when the imperialist nations ran on their own swords.

For the British the objective after 1898 was how to secure its highly favored position in east Asia as rivalry with France, Germany, Russia, and Japan was heating up. For the Americans, in contrast, the purpose was a dual one and when compared to that of the British was more prudent and farsighted. Whereas London was wedded to the status quo because Britain enjoyed conspicuous advantages in China and was committed more to the exercise of power than its balance, the United States, reflecting the character of its own interests, found access to the China trade intimately bound up with a balance of power. Balanced power would work to prevent preemption from the Chinese commercial world. That the United States was intent on having a role in the Far East followed ineluctably from 1) Dewey's great victory at Manila; and 2) McKinley's decision to retain the whole of the Philippine archipelago.

As stunning as was Dewey's destruction of the Spanish fleet McKinley's action was altogether audacious, constituting as it does one of the most important diplomatic decisions in all of American history. The implications for American foreign policy for a long time to come no one could have measured at the time. Once Secretary of State Hay set forth the Open Door policy Anglo–American diplomatic relations took on an Asian cast.

In its pursuit of the status quo by means of superior power London became fixated by the prospect of a formal alliance with Japan and a de facto alliance with the United States, disguised as it might be. The pursuit of the former, the Anglo–Japanese connection deserves only limited attention here, yet Japan must be treated as a key element in Anglo-American Far Eastern diplomacy in the first years of the twentieth century. Down to 1907 the Foreign Office had two bêtes noires: Germany and Russia. Due to the exertions of Sir Edward Grey who succeeded as foreign minister when the Liberals came to power the Russian devil was exorcised and the Triple Entente: England, France, and Russia, became a reality. Before that date, however, Britain feared Russian machinations in Persia, and more to the point, like activities in Manchuria. These latter moves were presumed to be a threat because Russian presence and investments were significant and were growing. The Japanese who had an exploitive eye on Manchuria also felt directly threatened by Russia; the two powers might conceivably go to war over control of Manchuria. By aligning itself with the world's mightiest empire Tokyo was convinced it had executed a diplomatic coup. Of course, not a few of the more cunning people in the Foreign Office might have been buoyed up by the prospect that the Japanese could do their fighting for them if it did come to war in the East not over the China trade but the China spoils.

United States Stake. Apart from British involvement in the Far East the State Department recognized from the outset, from the take-over of the Philippines, that Japan had to be figured into American diplomatic strategy for that part of the globe. It is equally true Tokyo soon realized there was a new and important player in the scramble for a slice of the China trade, one that was on the threshold of becoming the giant of the industrial world. Would the two nations clash or cooperate? Such a question must be posed in all seriousness even though it was likely that they could get on together as early as 1905 or 1908, the dates respectively of the Taft-Katsura and the Root-Takahira agreements. Rather it was because it was to Great Britain's advantage to build on the assumption that Washington and Tokyo, having a common friend in London, could therefore, be friends themselves. Such an understanding operated on the consideration there was to be no clash of vital interests between or among the three powers. And that was in fact the case; cooperation was workable. This skeletonlike analysis must now be fleshed out.

With the United States esconced on the periphery of the Asian mainland by reason of possessing the Philippines it did not take a visionary to appreciate Manila could become a great entrepot of trade and commerce should the Americans decide to participate in the economic development of China. As has been noted the British were keen to have the United States "associate" with them in determining the present as well as the future state of China. As early as March 1898, before the start of the Spanish American War, Lord Pauncefote approached Secretary of State John Sherman, sounding out the possibility of Anglo-American cooperation. Implicitly, Pauncefote was asking Washington to support an open door policy. The proposal, tendered again in January of the next year, was not acted upon by the McKinley administration. The conventional procedures having produced negative results informal diplomacy took over.

Background to the Open Door. Lord Charles Beresford had spent years in the Far East, and had come forth with a book, *The Breakup of China*. It quickly became a major reference point for leaders in England and America when they contemplated the future of the Asiatic land mass. By means of a number of speeches delivered in major cities in the United States Beresford managed to energize American interest in the future of China. Even the State Department was brought round to considering seriously why the United States should be thinking along geopolitical lines and how the McKinley administration might proceed. The wheels of informal diplomacy now began to run faster. A. E. Hippesley, a British subject and an old China hand was a close friend of W. W. Rockhill who, in turn, was a trusted advisor to Secretary Hay when it came to Chinese affairs. Hippesley had been a member of the Chinese Maritime Customs Service and knew the conditions in the country thoroughly. Of course he was always on the lookout to find ways to protect Great Britain's dominant position in matters of Far Eastern trade. One third of foreign investments in China were British and 80 percent of the shipping of goods was in British hands. Rockhill as an American was one of the few of his countrymen who had mastered the Chinese language and knew its culture. He had been second secretary of the legation in Peking after 1884, the year he met and became friendly with Hippesley. Their common bond was the belief that Great Britain and the United States would each do well were they to take a united stand on the open door. This was most likely to be achieved on the American side by enlisting the active support of Rockhill's friend, John Hay. London, of course, had no problem with the open door, indeed, wanted it to be the operating principle of trade in China. Britain feared its secure holdings in China were about to be threatened by the establishment of various leaseholds, given by Peking to rival powers. Under these arrangements leaseholders were granted investment privileges and political concessions under the rules of extraterritoriality. If London could convince Washington to endorse the open door principle both countries could profit.

In as much as Rockhill had not been in China for several years and was somewhat rusty as to details of the situation there and Hippesley was fresh from the scene it fell to the latter to compose a memorandum, advancing his ideas of commercial equality. After some revisions entered by Rockhill it was presented to President McKinley. This occurred in August 1899. The next month John Hay issued what has come to be termed the first Open Door Note, cloned from the Hippesley memorandum as revised by Rockhill as approved by the president. At this latter juncture formal diplomacy took over, the Open Door was declared American policy. In the judgment of one leading authority, "thus the British succeeded in committing the United States to a policy favorable to their Chinese interests." But this statement must be viewed in its long term consequences rather than its short term reception. Reaction in America was tentatively favorable owing to a limited understanding and concern of both politicians and the public. In fact its biggest appeal was that it appeared to serve the cause of peace and civilization, because American trade with China, amounting to less that 2 percent of total United States commerce, was so insignificant. As for the reception in Britain feelings were mixed. Lord Salisbury liked the fact of the open door, but was not so keen on the pronouncement because it might restrict the expansion of British trade in areas of China beyond where it already obtained. (*See Document No. 15.*)

First Open Door Note. Washington had now gone public with its announcement which, upon examination, revealed it was much less sweeping than it was made to sound. Spheres of influence were treated as existing facts, no reference was made to mining or railroad concessions, or of investment capital. The only specific concerned equal commercial opportunities. In issuing the note Hay was asking for assurances of agreement from all the powers with holdings in China. In its exact form the British came to understand there was little to fear and probably something to gain. According to Lord Salisbury the Open Door Note was "a work of great importance and utility to the world, and especially to our respective countries." John Hay came away pleased that the cause of Anglo-Americanism was so well served. (*See Document Nos. 16 and 17.*)

Second Open Door Note. The Boxer Rebellion of 1900 was short lived as it was put down with brutal force by a composite of foreign troops, including units from Britain, Japan, Russia, and the United States. The uprising simply had no chance of rescuing China from its vulnerable decrepitude. On the contrary the presence of these various military units from countries anxious to exploit resources and control the Chinese economy might portend an era of quasi-colonization as spheres of influence became leaseholds and these in turn began to look more and more like possessions. With China on the brink of partition Secretary Hay in July 1900, issued a second Open Door Note, at the core of which was a singular piece of American diplomacy. If it was at the time a policy without teeth, this is not to argue that it could not grow teeth in the years to come. Openly but not defiantly it proclaimed the American intention of seeking to guarantee the territorial and administrative integrity of the beleaguered Chinese nation. No one, including Hay, could have begun to calculate the influence of this policy over the course of the whole of the twentieth century. At the moment, it won the support of important circles in Britain; *The Times* asserted that "it was more clear than ever before that the main interests of the United States and Great Britain are at present identical." It was another example of the improvement of Anglo-American diplomatic cooperation. John Hay was more than ever certain, except for American domestic politics with its combination of anti-imperialist and anti-British sentiment, the United States "could and should join with England and make our ideals prevail." Such an assessment tends to underscore that as Anglophilic as

John Hay was, and as important as his position in the American government, events, even seemingly extraneous events, might have a way of affecting and determining policy. (*See Document No. 18.*)

If London welcomed the second Open Door Note the Japanese, about to be cultivated by the British, moves which would eventuate in the Anglo-Japanese Treaty, were apprehensive about their future role in China. The final text of the treaty stated support for equality of commercial opportunity (the point of Hay's first announcement) and provided for the maintenance of Chinese territorial integrity (the leading consideration of Hay's second note). American policy was obviously gaining acknowledgement. Lord Lansdowne was able to reassure the Japanese the United States would be amenable to this new alliance of east and west. Ambassador Choate, speaking in London to the press lords and the noble lords, concurred in Lansdowne's judgment. As of 1902 Anglo-American and Anglo-Japanese diplomacy was maintaining a steady and friendly course. This proved to be but a temporary state of affairs.

Russo-Japanese War. In the swirling eddies of international politics after 1898 it sometimes requires a steady eye to remain trained on British-American diplomacy to see it as a matter of Anglo-American cooperation. The outbreak of war between Russia and Japan in 1904 is a persuasive example. It is also another instance in which informal diplomacy had a leading role. The origins of the war were in the tangled web of rivalry in China. Both the Russians and the Japanese were intent on controlling Manchuria for commercial as well as military reasons. A natural rivalry, it exploded into war when Japan suddenly attacked Russian holdings in the disputed region. As a treaty ally Britain at the outset considered its fortunes tied to Japanese success. Thus London and Washington could hardly undertake a common approach to a short war and a quick peace. What occurred instead was a series of informal exchanges between President Roosevelt and some of his well placed English friends, chief among whom was Cecil Spring Rice. Such privately circulated letters add an important dimension to diplomacy in action.

Roosevelt Steps In. In the negotiations leading up to the Treaty of Portsmouth, which brought an end to the Russo-Japanese War, Roosevelt demonstrated a sense of national interest, as the British conceived their own to be, in Downing Street's refusal to facilitate the president's efforts to conclude the conflict. Great Britain as an ally of Japan was in a position to exert some pressure on her Asian friend, had it looked upon this as strengthening Far Eastern prospects. On the contrary, for a long time it hoped for a sweeping Japanese victory, judging this to be the way best designed to meet its needs. Roosevelt preferred to balance an emerging Japan against an established Russia, partly because he feared an all powerful Japan as a threat to the United States in that area of the world. As a result of this diverging appreciation of the implications inherent in the war, TR got little encouragement so long as it seemed Japan would win a decisive victory. When after a series of stunning triumphs over Russia in 1904 and 1905 Tokyo found the nation facing bankruptcy, then and only then did Britain begin to support peace efforts. In May 1905, for example, Spring Rice came to Washington to act as a special/unofficial intermediary between the president and the foreign minister. But there was no meeting of the Anglo-American minds. By the midsummer London had begun to alter its outlook. Spring Rice, returned to his post in Russia, wrote that the object of England was to see peace established. He added that Lord Lansdowne was prepared to wait for "the right time" and that any American initiative would be given the fullest and friendliest consideration. Within another month this guarded expression of hope had altered in tone and substance. Spring Rice was prepared to tell the president Lansdowne strongly supported TR's role as peacemaker, and that it was London's view it was in Japan's best interest to get out of the war quickly. Nonetheless a disagreement on timing did not lead to a falling out between London and Washington. Official channels of communication did not dry up completely while semiofficial lines of communication remained constantly in use. These considerations were illustrated by Roosevelt's comments to Arthur Hamilton Lee in September 1905, as the British were in the process of reaffirming their Japanese alliance. The president wrote: "I have been shown the rough draft of the treaty . . . I think it is a very good thing for England and Japan, and I think it is a decidedly good thing for the United States and the rest of the world." Bear in mind, Lee was not a Foreign Office official, a member of Parliament only, but a friend of Theodore Roosevelt. He also wrote in much the same vein to St. Loe Strachey, editor of the influential journal, *The Spectator.*

The president's letters to and from his friends in London, as these touched on the Russo-Japanese War are valuable for the sidelights thrown on the Anglo-American way of viewing common interests. As such they tend to confirm the importance of informal diplomacy. Throughout his correspondence the president took occasion to reassure his English friends that his policy, aimed at bringing about peace, was not anti-British. but he was not above expressing his annoyance. At one time he chided Spring Rice for what he termed "needless heroics" respecting the Englishman's contention that his country's "honor commanded her to abstain from persuading the Japanese to halt the war." And he went on: "I wholly fail to see the difference in position which makes it proper for France, the ally of Russia, to urge Russia to make peace and which yet makes it improper for England, the ally of Japan, to urge Japan to make peace." What the president really desired was a joint Anglo-American policy toward all matters pertaining to Japan, including mass Japanese migrations to the United States and the Commonwealth countries in the Pacific. Once the Treaty of Portsmouth had been signed in 1906 the informal diplomats were altogether congratulatory. Spring Rice put it this way: "the president singlehandedly effected a peace, against the wishes of the Japanese people (there was no huge indemnity leveled against Russia as was popularly demanded) and the Russian government (forced to give up half of Shaklin [sic] Island, to which it reluctantly agreed)." This assessment typified the view of Roosevelt's English correspondents. (*See Document No. 19.*)

Agreements Follow. Once the second Anglo-Japanese Treaty (1905) had been signed British relations with Japan could fall into a settled channel. In keeping within the tenor of mutual need and respect the United States, even as the Russo-Japanese War continued to be waged, negotiated a parallel kind of agreement with Tokyo, the Taft-Katsura Memorandum. True enough it was to bind only the Roosevelt administration. Depending on who TR's successor in office would be, and of course it turned out to be Taft himself, both London and Tokyo could probably count on the same spirit of need and respect to prevail amongst the three nations. By terms of the Taft-Katsura Agreement the Japanese forswore any aggressive designs on the American held Philippines; in return the United States affirmed Japan's "suzerainty" over Korea. It was about this time Roosevelt wrote Taft that in his judgment the Philippine Islands could prove to be an Achilles heel, a metaphor but a revealing one because it conveyed the idea that the United States power was likely overextended in the Far East. Nevertheless London had

reason to rejoice at the Taft-Katsura Agreement because it greatly less-
ened the prospect of confrontation between its Asian ally and its American friend. To have to choose between Tokyo and Washington is something no British minister could contemplate with an easy mind. (*See
Document No. 20.*) Three years later, in 1908 a second exchange of notes
led to the Root-Takahira Agreement. Major provisions, including the
maintenance of the status quo in the region, upholding the open door
in China and the preservation of Chinese integrity resonated well not
only in Britain and the United States but on the European continent as
well. When informed of the terms of the agreement, Sir Edward Grey
summed up the British response in simple terms: "we were very pleased
with it, because we ourselves were especially desirous of remaining on
good terms with the United States." This interpretation amounts to a
masterpiece of English understatement because, after all, it signified the
Japanese and Americans were willing to support Great Britain's advantageous position in the Far East. (*See Document No. 21.*)

Other moves by the Roosevelt administration that were peculiarly
American disturbed the calm waters only slightly. One of these was the
controversy sparked by the segregation of children of Oriental ancestry
by the San Francisco School Board. Fundamentally this action spoke
the fear and resentment Californians felt over the increasingly large
number of immigrants from Japan. At first the London government
deemed the Americans utterly wrong headed in the matter, always bear-
ing in mind the sensitivities of its ally. But when the Canadians, particularly with regard to immigration into Vancouver, took the same attitude as the Americans, Grey was on the horns of a dilemma from which
he was barely able to free himself. He lent a sympathetic ear to the government in Ottawa and hoped the controversy would die down. A second minor issue between Washington and London was the round
the world voyage of the Great White Fleet (1908). The brain child of
Theodore Roosevelt, as he saw it, it was a way of ringing down the
curtain on his presidential diplomacy as sixteen armored battleships
ploughed their way across the Pacific. Grey feared it might be interpreted as a provocation: what would the Japanese make of it? Would an
incident or an accident occasion ill will? On the contrary, the voyage was
a great success. The welcome given the fleet in Sydney was overwhelm-
ing and the Japanese could not have been more receptive in their official
welcome. After that London breathed more easily and this was reflected
as the fleet passed through the straits of Gibraltar. As Roosevelt took

leave of office in March 1909, the Anglo-American Far Eastern policies had coalesced and in ways pleasing to both governments.

TR: Power Broker Again. Further appreciation of the deepening American involvement in world politics and of American success in conflict resolution may be gleaned from President Roosevelt's role in arranging the Algeciras Conference of 1905–1906. Essentially a conflict between France and Germany over hegemony in Morocco it nevertheless had implications for Anglo-American friendship. Perhaps it merits only limited attention here, yet it clearly shows Roosevelt's concern for the success of the recently created Anglo-French Entente (1904). England had decided to cast its fortune with the age-old enemy, France, to counter the growing power of a potential enemy, Germany. In other words the president believed the entente was a vital factor in keeping the peace in Europe, and thereby in the world. Roosevelt acted at Germany's request for a conference to be called, but only after he was able to put aside his self-doubts as to whether the United States should be in any way involved. America had no vital interest in that part of the world, and was not likely to develop one. When TR announced his intention to arrange a meeting of concerned parties the British were cool to the whole idea. Only slowly was it realized in the Foreign Office that the entente with France might be in jeopardy with Germany seeking to drive a wedge between Paris and London. From the outset, Roosevelt was clearly on the French side, but he strove, at the same time, to appear to be neutral. His appointment of Henry White, the veteran diplomat, as the American representative at the conference was perfect for that arrangement. As issue after issue was addressed White's was the voice of moderation, and it was generally realized, except perhaps in the British press, that the American purpose was to help preserve the entente. As Secretary of State Root had instructed White: "we regard as a favorable condition for the peace of the world, and therefore the best interests of the United States, the continued entente cordiale between France and England, and we do not wish to contribute toward any estrangement between the two nations." White had taken Root's instructions and had translated them into a successful piece of diplomacy, much to Britain's advantage, however slowly the Foreign Office came to appreciate it. Probably because Roosevelt did not trumpet the American intentions and their implementation, there grew to be a certain hostility or at least suspicion toward Roosevelt himself, as noted in the Lon-

don newspapers. But once the facts were known with the dispersal of
the conferees he quickly returned to the good graces of the English
press and people. Arthur Lee wrote to this effect in a letter to the president in March 1907. "I doubt if there is any responsible person left over
here who harbours delusions anymore about your alleged anti-British
stance." Nor, given all the facts, should there have been.

Swettenham Incident. On January 14, 1907 a devastating earthquake struck Kingston, the capital city of Jamaica and fire completed
the ruin of the town. The loss of life, some estimates placed the number
at two thousand, and the destruction of property created a chaos with
local authorities overwhelmed. Help from whatever quarter was needed
and needed immediately. In addition to sending messages of condolence
to the British government and to King Edward VII, the United States
stood ready to do what it could to alleviate the distress. The British con-
sul general in Havana called on the civil and naval authorities there to
offer aid, and the Navy responded almost at once, sending a total of four
ships with men and supplies. All this was conveyed to the Foreign Secretary by the British chargé d'affaires at the Washington embassy.
Meanwhile on January 17 the Congress passed a resolution authorizing
the provision of food, clothing and medicine. Admiral Charles Davis
was placed in charge of this mission of mercy, as the ships left Guan-
tanomo in Cuba for Kingston. There seemed to be no dispute that time
was of the essence and thus the support provided truly lifesaving. The
colonial governor of Jamaica, Alexander Swettenham was, however, to
prove a stumbling block. It is hard to explain his less than appreciative
response to the assistance given except as a matter of personal pique,
fed by his anti-Americanism.

In two ways in particular the American actions greatly troubled the
governor. The first was he had issued no official invitation or permission
to the United States to send help, and therefore the arrival of the Americans was highly irregular, a violation of international law and practice.
Bear in mind that the people of Jamaica were crying for assistance and
given the degree of their misery indifferent as to its source. The second
particular was the landing of armed sailors from the battleship *Missouri*
on sovereign British soil, and without the governor's permission. It was
to his way of thinking an act of war. Yet the people were glad to see the
Americans whose mission it was to proceed to the island prison and

there to make sure the six hundred inmates did not mutiny and turning on their captors cause more death and destruction. The American sailors, numbering less than one hundred officers and men, kept that situation under control.

Both Swettenham and Davis filed numerous reports of happenings as they saw them but between them there were sharp disagreements. Both the Foreign Office and the State Department were disturbed by Swettenham's assertion of American impropriety and especially to the governor's charges of illegalities and acts of war. Newspapers on both sides of the Atlantic, after giving full coverage to the earthquake and fires, turned their attention to the diplomatic controversy. Swettenham had few supporters, but he made up for this with his bluster over what he termed high-handed American behavior. He had virtually no ally in the Foreign Office, and Grey was acutely embarrassed by his threat to publish a "full report." Both Washington and London hoped the whole episode would end quietly but Swettenham was not to be put aside and silenced easily. It truly was a tempest in a tea pot, as the pot kept boiling away. President Roosevelt was as disturbed as anyone, not by the governor's lack of grace and gratitude, but by his contention that the United States navy had committed a war-like act. In the end, or by July 1907, Swettenham was retired from the colonial service at the insistence of Lord Elgin, colonial secretary, but not before threatening his own government with self-serving exposé.

Incident in Perspective. Was the Swettenham affair, taken all in all, of any significance in the ongoing growth of Anglo-American accord? The answer might well be: yes and no. At its heart the controversy centered on a point of honor, which in itself had the potential for growing into a major confrontation. On the other hand, such was the rapport that had been achieved between the two English-speaking nations that the ill will of one low ranked civil servant was hardly the incident of which diplomatic crises are made. In 1895 there had been a fire at Port of Spain in Trinidad, British at the time, which wiped out much of the town. American sailors were landed to help put out the fire and the governor of Trinidad wrote of his heartfelt thanks for the timely presence of these United States service men. Had his response in 1895 been that of Governor Swettenham, a year when British-American relations were less than friendly, the fallout might have been severe enough to render impossible a peaceful settlement of the Venezuelan boundary dispute. By 1907, however, such was the cordiality and understanding and the trust prevailing between the two nations Swettenham could hardly be taken seriously. By way of a lesson the whole affair goes to demonstrate both to domestic opponents of rapprochement and foreign observers as well that the special relationship was now definitely confirmed.

CHAPTER 5

CHANGING THE GUARD

New Leaders. The departure of Theodore Roosevelt from the White House in March 1909, represents something of a dividing line for the early years of the special relationship. He had wanted to leave a legacy of cooperation between Washington and London and in that respect had succeeded, despite some rough patches that put a strain on the goodwill of the two nations. Beyond that, TR had every reason to believe his friend and successor, William Howard Taft, would be well disposed toward Britain, and he was entirely correct. His confidence was based on Taft's judicious temperament and his natural Anglophilia. At bottom Taft was a student and practitioner of American law, the origins of which he believed could be traced to the common law of old England. Nor, as it happened need Roosevelt have had reason to worry about the like disposition of Taft's successor in the presidency, Woodrow Wilson. All four of Wilson's grandparents had been born in the British Isles. Gladstone was Wilson's earliest political hero, and he was a lifetime admirer of Wordsworth's poetry. Taft and Wilson were truly like-minded when it came to sympathy for England and things English. At the same time both men were fundamentally American when it came to policy and its implementation. Neither had the bravura quality of Roosevelt yet their lack of a florid style was incidental to their insistence on looking after the vital interests of the United States when it came to Anglo–American diplomacy. This emphasis on the diplomacy of Taft and Wilson in the period, 1909–1914, is appropriate because the major problems that emerged in those years saw the Americans take the offensive, to which the British were prone only to react. Add to this the fact that Sir Edward Grey was in charge of the Foreign Office from 1908 to 1916, a statesman who was profoundly pro-American, the appearance as well as the reality were centered in initiatives by the United States. The thinking in London was that America was a wholly reliable friend whereas Grey's real worries were in Europe and the Empire.

New Problems. Two important problems surfaced with which Taft, Wilson, and Grey had to concern themselves in the years down to 1914. One of these was the prospect of arbitration by treaty arrangement between Great Britain and United States, which if successfully negotiated would close off for good any idea of war between the two sovereignties. The second issue was the matter of equal tolls to be charged for the passage of ships through the Panama Canal, scheduled for opening in 1914. At the time both these problems loomed large but they never stood out as divisive despite serious disagreements between London and Washington. Also to be considered were United States-Mexican relations, of concern to the British because of heavy investments in Mexico and therefore of worry about revolutions in Mexico, with threats to British owned property. Finally, the exchange of new ambassadors needs to be addressed, if for no other reason than they were to play key roles in high level diplomacy during World War I. Wilson's choice for the London post was Walter Hines Page, an inveterate Anglophile. Grey was to second Cecil Spring Rice, pro-American but not to a fault.

New Times. It is ironic indeed that with the onset of the twentieth-century European civilization—"the West" in other words, thereby including the United States within its meaning—there hung over the period an earnest desire for peace and an equally earnest preparation for war. In 1901 the decision remained unresolved as to which would prevail, peace or war. The sinews of war were all too familiar, the paths of peace less well known but real enough nevertheless. As a matter of function, arbitration of issues between and among the great powers was synonymous with peace. Despite the eventual failure of arbitration, the rejection of it really, as a substitute for and an antidote to contending armies, 1914–1918 and all its lugubrious consequences, the West was alive with optimism. Creation of the Courts of International Justice at The Hague seemed to say as much. In addition there was a League for Peace organized in the United States and strongly supported by that son of the British Isles who made his fortune in America, Andrew Carnegie. Most important was concrete evidence arbitration was a workable proposition. Certainly no two nations had striven harder to make arbitration a viable alternate than had Great Britain and the United States.

Unfortunately "peace" was easily transmuted to "pacifism" and to some leaders in both countries pacifism was a dirty word. It spoke a willingness to abandon interests, considered vital to a nation, to a body of supposedly neutral observers. Roosevelt dismissed such men as "foreigners." Pacifism implied that "the fighting edge" had grown dull, too dull to protect such interests. Pacifists were effete, if not decadent. Pacifism and national honor were contradictions in terms. Therefore any effort to bring about a genuine treaty of arbitration between Great Britain and the United States would have to overcome the undertow of nationalism, which upon consideration, must be estimated as the most powerful and persuasive force to be found in nineteenth century Western civilization. World War I is grim evidence of this.

Taft and Arbitration. No leader, either American or British, pursued the quest for a treaty of arbitration more diligently or devotedly than President Taft. Writing to his military aide, Archie Butt, in April 1911, Taft pointed out that a genuine arbitration treaty "will be the great jewel of my administration. But just as it will be the greatest act during these four years, it will also be the greatest failure if I do not get it ratified." For the president the timing seemed right. The Pelagic sealing question was disposed of by an international conference of four nations. Designed to preserve the seal herds of the North Pacific the agreement favored the American position. More germane to his hopes was the means used to settle the Newfoundland fishing dispute. Under a general treaty of arbitration (1908) Secretary of State Root had arranged for the submission of questions to the Permanent Court of Arbitration at The Hague, and the decision rendered by that tribunal was accepted by London and Washington. Similarly a final boundary line between Canada and the United States, including questions arising about the use of waterways along the boundary, was to be settled by the working of a joint commission. It is understandable in light of all this activity why Taft wanted to seize the day and push for groundbreaking arbitration treaties beginning with Britain. The prospects for success were enhanced by the outlook of Sir Edward Grey and the enthusiasm of HM ambassador to Washington, James Bryce. (*See Document No. 22.*)

Taft was consistent, bold, and unambiguous in stating publicly the sweep of his vision when promoting the idea. As early as February 1910, he came out four square as an advocate of peaceful rather than warlike solutions to issues dividing his nation from Britain. "I have noticed exceptions in our arbitration treaties to date as to reference of questions of honor, of national honor, to courts of arbitration. Personally I don't see why matters of national honor should not be referred to a court any more than matters of property or of proprietorship. . . . I do not see why questions of national honor may not be submitted to a tribunal com-

posed of men of honor who understand questions of national honor."
Taft repeated this message time after time as he campaigned for public
support for his dream of world peace. It was clear from his many statements Taft was aiming for nothing less than arbitration of international
disputes in the full meaning of the term.

This meaning is readily identified in the text of the proposed treaty.
The preamble stated its purpose: to "provide means for the peaceful
solution of all questions of difference which it should in the future be
found to be impossible to settle by diplomacy." Article I, the most sub-
stantive, held that differences between the high contracting parties "relating to matters which are justiciable in their nature by reason of being
susceptible of decision by application of the principles of equity and justice, should be referred either to the Court of Arbitration at The Hague
or to some other arbitral tribunal as may be decided in each case by
special agreement." This was indeed an all encompassing provision.

The Senate Says No. Diplomatic conversations opened in January 1911, between President Taft and the British ambassador. Within
two months as a result of discussions between Bryce and Secretary of
State Philander Knox a preliminary draft was prepared. By May 1
Washington had approved this draft whereupon it was delivered to the
Foreign Office for cabinet approval. Both Liberals and Conservatives in
the House of Commons lent it support. The business of the treaty was
moving at an unusually rapid pace. Bryce and Knox signed the final version on August 3, 1911. For London arbitration under treaty rules was
a done deal. Yet once again the United States Senate was to have the last
word. Debate involving the principles of arbitration and the specifics of
the treaty under consideration commenced in the early autumn of that
year, extending into the spring of 1912. The result of Senate action may
be summed up in one word: evisceration. The senators insisted on exceptions if the treaty was to be put into effect: issues affecting the laws
of immigration of the United States and its States' educational systems,
any question treating territorial integrity, the Monroe Doctrine, and
"other purely governmental policy." What had been intended as a model
arbitration treaty and were other nations to sign it, was seen as a major
step in the direction of world peace, had fallen victim to American nationalism and ultimately tossed aside. The president, sorely distressed
by the outcome, had no choice but to refuse to send the Senate version
to London for consideration. The treaty in effect was dead. Admittedly,

it is questionable to argue that one arbitration agreement between two nations already on the friendliest terms could have averted the cataclysm of the Great War. But given its fate it does not seem excessive to maintain that arbitration as a *modus operandi* for settling major international differences was doomed.

For the British the show was over as increasingly, beginning in 1912, Grey was preoccupied with Balkan wars, naval and army build-ups, and German ambitions in Asia Minor. The new Wilson administration coming into office in March 1913, was well disposed toward peaceful solutions of even the most dangerous international crisis, by reason of the president's public philosophy as applied to world affairs and that of his secretary of state, William Jennings Bryan. By this date Bryan was a full blown pacifist. He sought and gained approval of the Senate to extend the very tame and irresolute arbitration agreement of 1908. Furthermore he attempted to advance a treaty of his own devising, one of the features of which called for a year's cooling off period to avert a diplomatic confrontation from becoming a war. One ranking Foreign Office authority dismissed it as too theoretical and too visionary but Grey was willing to sign the agreement in September, 1914. It was only a month before when Sir Edward addressed the House of Commons with his often-cited lament: the lights were going out all over the world and might not be lighted again in a lifetime. The principle of arbitration had a pitiless destiny.

Canal Tolls. Construction of the canal across the isthmus of Panama had proceeded steadily after 1904. Within less than ten years the completion of this enormous undertaking was in sight, a consideration prompting discussion about the tolls which would be charged American ships as well as those of foreign registry. As early as December 1910, President Taft in his annual message to Congress initiated discussion of what was soon to be a burning issue. Among other aspects of the future use of the canal the president wanted American ships engaged in coastwise commerce exempted from paying a toll. According to Taft, this amounted to nothing more than a subsidy to American merchant shipping, just as other countries subsidized their merchantmen in a variety of ways. Thereafter Taft grew more convinced this was the right and proper way to proceed. As he told the Congress on another occasion: "We own the canal, it was our money that built it, we have the right to charge tolls as we see fit." The congress hardly needed any encouragement and in 1912 passed legislature specifically exempting American coastwise shippers from paying tolls.

British Reaction. Reaction in England to the law was an instantaneous uproar. The United States was accused of bad faith, nay of dishonor. The American ambassador reported from London: "Everywhere—in circles the most friendly to us and the most informed—I receive communications because of the dishonorable attitude of our Government about the Canal Tolls." And apparently he was not exaggerating in describing the British mood. At times in the not so distant past such terms as "bad faith" and "dishonor" would have been fighting words. But this was 1912 and the undergirding of the rapprochement was strong enough to preclude any chance of resorting to force.

What particularly was the reason for British outrage? Very simply the exact wording of the 1901 Hay–Pauncefote Treaty. The crucial part read as follows: "The canal shall be free and open to the vessels of commerce and of war of all nations . . . and there shall be no discrimination against any nation . . . in respect of the conditions or charges of traffic or otherwise." The statement seems plain enough in its intent. The American interpretation was that the meaning intended was "of all other nations" in as much as the Americans owned the canal. Yet the word "other" was never used, and one may presume it was not inserted because it was inappropriate . . . in 1901. This view was widely held in the United States: all three candidates for the presidency in 1912 took that line of argument. It should be noted the issue did not involve a vital interest of either Britain or the United States but a bandying about of such phrases as bad faith and dishonor could be unpredictably incendiary. How was the issue to be resolved?

Wilson's Solution. President Wilson who had not studied the matter closely as he fought his election campaign was willing to reconsider the matter, once he was safely in office. Even so, he was not prepared to take it under serious advisement until certain key domestic legislation, especially the Federal Reserve Act as well as preliminaries to the passing of the Clayton Anti-Trust Act, were completed. His ambassador in London, Walter Hines Page, urged him to study the matter carefully to place it in the larger context of Anglo-American affairs. But for Wilson the strong argument for repealing the 1912 exemption law was a moral one: American honor, Americans were as good as their word.

Passing the law had been easy; repealing it would become much more difficult, if for no other reason than it came down to a change of policy, a policy the Congress would have to admit was wrong. Wilson failed to persuade two leading Democrats, Champ Clark of Missouri who was Speaker of the House and Oscar Underwood of Alabama, the party majority leader. The Tammany contingent was opposed as well as the Irish-American representatives, to whom should be added a few Anglophobe Republicans. After serious debate the House of Representatives voted 247 to 162 for repeal. A prolonged debate in the Senate followed, with the tally 50 to 35 for repeal. As insulted and betrayed as the English press and public felt, the government, including both Prime Minister H. H. Asquith and foreign secretary Grey, refused to be drawn into recriminations. From the outset both insisted it was "absolutely clear" the United States had pledged equity in the matter of tolls but American friendship was too highly valued to be allowed to be weakened for a light or transient reason.

Mexico: Economy and Politics. Grey, and therefore the British government, strove to maintain a similar attitude of patient detachment regarding United States policy toward Mexico in the early months of the Wilson administration. The possibility of a rupture was present but the foreign secretary guarded against it, putting accord with America as a high priority. At the start of the twentieth century Mexico was a country recognized as rich in natural resources with its petroleum reserves among its most obvious assets. Ruled over by a succession of dictator presidents its form of government left a great deal to be desired for an idealist such as President Wilson. The previous Taft administration had, however, adjusted to the need of dealing with a corrupt government as long as it was stable enough to protect American investments which stood at over $2 billion. Mexico was a beneficiary and also a victim of Dollar diplomacy, the leitmotif of Taft's foreign policy. Along side American capital, and in ways competing with it, were heavy British investments. The British attitude toward dealing with venal politicians was undistinguishable from that of the Americans. As long as law and order were maintained and profits continued to flow out of Mexico how the country was governed was immaterial. Foreign investments aside, a political crisis had developed toward the close of the Taft administration. The corrupt President Porfirio Diaz was being challenged by an idealistic reformer, Francisco Madero. Twenty thousand American troops were massed along the Mexico-American border in case of wide-spread civil disturbances. The United States and Great Britain were apprehensive both as to what was happening at the moment and what it might mean for the security of foreign owned property in the long run. Diaz abdicated his power in 1911, to be succeeded by Madero who, though popular with the people, was unable to govern. He was soon ousted from power by General Victoriano Huerta, and subsequently killed. Huerta by that act was perceived by President Wilson as a man with blood on his hands. Such was the state of affairs in Mexico when Wilson came into office in 1913. The question being asked in London and in Washington was how much property risk was there under the new regime. Huerta appeared to promise law and order, Diaz style, and the British government without consulting with the United States, extended diplomatic recognition to the Huerta regime. That move caused at least a ripple on the waters of Anglo-American affairs. The British by word and deed had already conceded to the United States the role of policeman of the western hemisphere and were content with that as it applied to Mexico. In retrospect it would have been wise to have consulted the United States before giving Huerta a seal of approval. Events were heightening President Wilson's scorn for Huerta. He was appalled by the ordered execution of Madero and withheld recognition of the new government. Wilson wanted a promise of free elections as a first condition to be met. Beneath the surface of these public events was competition between the two English-speaking nations for control of the oil fields. The Admiralty, more and more reliant on oil to power its ships, was especially supportive of English efforts in this respect. Of course Standard Oil was interested as well. Wilson was unrelenting in his opposition to Huerta. When questioned by the British diplomat, Sir William Tyrrell, about the intentions of his Mexican policy, the president replied that he wanted to teach the Mexicans to elect good men. It was an assertion some Foreign Office people deemed "quixotic" as well it may have been. But it was pure Woodrow Wilson, centered on morality rather than real politik. Despite infighting at home Grey held consistently to the line that Mexico was in the United States sphere of influence, and he would conduct diplomacy accordingly. "His Majesty's Government," Grey argued, "can not with any prospect of success embark upon an action counter to the policy of that of the United States." Yet he had chosen as the minister to the new Huerta government Sir Lionel Cardon, who suffered from a severe case of Yankeephobia. When

Wilson was apprised of this he wrote a stinging rebuke to the foreign secretary but did not actually despatch the letter on the advice of John Bassett Moore, a senior State Department counsellor. Taking the advice of Grey Cardon began to moderate his anti-Americanism, and soon thereafter was sent into retirement, to which he did not submit gracefully. In the midst of all this the prime minister told a London audience that he was embracing a hands off policy toward Mexico. Anglo-American relations regarding Mexico improved to the point where American military personnel would soon be protecting British-owned property south of the Rio Grande. The United States continued to be embroiled with Mexico itself but on the diplomatic front London had bowed out.

With the advent of the Wilson administration, but without forebodings of the importance of the character of men who would be ambassadors between the two nations, Anglo-American diplomacy had reached a rare level of intimacy. This called for the appointment of individuals who truly did understand and appreciate the cultures as well as the public policies of the country to which each was accredited. Grey chose as HM ambassador to Washington Cecil Spring Rice, an old Etonian who had been at Balliol when Grey had been a student. In that same year President Wilson sent Walter Hines Page to the Court of Saint James's as the United States envoy. If the American Embassy was not quite the premier station in the Diplomatic Service it was still very significant. The London position was however the most prestigious one the president could offer. That Spring Rice was thoroughly pro-American without ever losing sight of his responsibility to his own government while Page was completely sympathetic to England and its ways speaks volumes for the mutual trust and admiration the two governments enjoyed.

New Ambassadors. A word or two about the role/function of an ambassador must be offered. Ambassadors ordinarily do not deal with heads of state, but with subordinates, in this case with the foreign secretary (London) or the secretary of state (Washington). In extraordinary circumstances, wartime for example, they may have to deal with the prime minister or the president. The problem of ambassadors dealing with a head of state can be twofold: inferior to superior by reason of the office held; and as foreigners they may be required to press for actions which are considered at odds with the policies of the host government.

The British ambassador, Spring Rice, was a seasoned, professional diplomat, with impeccable credentials, and his Washington appointment was to be the climax of his long career. In 1886, after visiting a brother in Canada, he met Theodore Roosevelt on the eastern crossing of the Atlantic. In a short time they became fast friends. Roosevelt and his fiancée had decided to be married in London to avoid a New York society wedding, and Spring Rice stood as his best man. At that time a Foreign Office clerk Spring Rice applied for and received an appointment as a second secretary at the British embassy in Washington. A man of legendary charm, superbly educated, and the embodiment of a cultivated Englishman Spring Rice made many influential friends in the American capital, and before long he was invited to the famous Adams seminars, an off shoot of the salon Henry Adams maintained in the company of John Hay, Henry Cabot Lodge, Theodore Roosevelt, and others. Spring Rice liked Americans as much as Americans liked him. After his American assignment he was to occupy a variety of posts: Teheran, Cairo, Tokyo, St. Petersburg, Berlin, and Stockholm, the latter his first embassy. Despite this variety of exposures to foreign ways Spring Rice was deemed the leading American expert in Whitehall. Over the years he had kept up a steady correspondence with all sorts of important Americans, giving him easy access to those in power. All this paid off in 1913, even though poor health prevented him from entering actively on diplomatic business until 1914.

President Wilson named an old friend who was both a noted journalist and a man of affairs, but not a professional diplomat, to represent the United States in London. Walter Hines Page was a Southerner, as was Wilson, who had made his mark as an editor of the *Atlantic Monthly,* a magazine noted for its critical approach not only to literature but to public policy. Born on the eve of the Civil War in North Carolina he inherited from his father a loyalty to the Union, not uncommon for North Carolinians of the day. The cultural orientation of the Page family was thoroughly English so that it is possible to say that from an early age, rather much like Wilson, he was taught to admire the old mother country. As has been noted, two issues troubled Anglo-American relations in 1913-1914, the Panama tolls and events in Mexico. As to the first of these Page was a strong advocate of repeal of the 1912 law, and used his contacts with Colonel Edward M. House to make his arguments plain. But he certainly exaggerated when he contended that the tolls issue was "the most important thing for us on the diplomatic horizon." No doubt he was brought to say this because of his zeal for the justice of the British position. The Mexican matter was in fact more dangerous to harmony between the two countries because of the decision of the Foreign Office to make premature its recognition of the Huerta regime as the legitimate government. Page took it upon himself to convince the British of the earnestness of Wilson's resolve to hold Huerta accountable for his malicious behavior. Page read the Mexican situation exactly as did the president. It was Page who put Tyrrell in touch with important Americans in New York as part of his plan to persuade London to accede to American leadership; in so doing he helped to strengthen Sir Edward's hand with Foreign Office advisers. Page was proving himself to be skillful at diplomacy at least for the moment. When it came to the Great War he would have to handle far more numerous and far more delicate matters than tolls at Panama or revolutionaries in Mexico. From the start of the war the most difficult United States policy for Page to represent was President Wilson's pledge of strict neutrality. A study of the Page embassy will spell out this conflict, offering a sharp contrast between the conduct of British and American diplomacy as carried out through their respective ambassadors.

CHAPTER 6

WARTIME DIPLOMACY—BRITISH CONDUCT

The Men Involved. The formalities and much of the substance of Great Britain's wartime diplomacy as it related to the United States was literally in the hands of Cecil Spring Rice. Of course, diplomatic policy was formulated in London by the War Cabinet with the foreign secretary as the driving force down to his resignation in 1916. Such policy matters as affected the United States were to be articulated, explained, qualified and/or defended by HM ambassador. As it happened Grey and Spring Rice agreed not only in broad outline—according to Grey "the surest way to lose the war would be to antagonize Washington," a proposition with which the ambassador completely agreed—but also on most details. As a result the president and the State Department could be sure that what Spring Rice was saying in his representations to American officials was *mutatis mutandi* what the War Cabinet was thinking. By nature, by training and by experience Spring Rice was punctilious in the discharge of his duties; he rarely interspersed his own opinion should he disagree with London-made policy, so that he could be trusted by the people in the State Department with whom he worked. The ambassador saw it as his first duty to represent his government's views exactly.

President Woodrow Wilson was one to keep his own counsel. Except for early in the war Spring Rice's dealings with him were almost a matter of formalities. The president had limited confidence in professional diplomats, and even less in the amateur, including the American ambassador to London, Walter Hines Page. Perhaps because of his messianic complex, a characteristic Spring Rice identified early in their dealings, Wilson confided in few if any individuals. The one exception was Colonel Edward House and not even House could always be sure what Wilson was thinking on a given particular. It is understandable then the British envoy's influence with the president would be limited, despite getting off to a good start. This occurred in September 1914, when the German ambassador was putting out the story that Berlin was receptive to a negotiated peace but London was blocking the way. Spring Rice went directly to the president, providing him with the text of the Grey telegram disavowing what was termed a piece of German disinformation. Wilson was convinced, a good omen perhaps for future discussions of delicate matters sure to arise between England and America.

Declaration of London. The first serious divisive issue between London and Washington was the British refusal to abide by the provisions of the Declaration of London (1909). Neither nation had signed the document but it appealed to the Wilson administration as an expedient guideline. The main purpose of the Declaration had been to make it possible for neutral nations in time of war to trade with belligerents who were under blockade. For example, it provided a definition of contraband which would be favorable to a neutral trading nation such as the United States in selling certain materials to either side in a conflict. The Foreign Office rejected the American contention outright, whereupon Spring Rice advised his government of the dangers of alienating American good will by precipitous action. Robert Lansing, counsel to the State Department, set about drafting an equally abrupt reply, likely in turn, to antagonize the Foreign Office. Were Lansing's letter to be received, unrevised, Spring Rice predicted the jolting effect would be greater than that caused by President Cleveland's 1895 message over the Venezuelan boundary line. He expressed the wish that Lansing tone down his rhetoric and at the same time advised Grey to be patient. This tactic was soon to become a standard procedure for Spring Rice, that of urging reconsideration on both parties when there was serious disagreement. Spring Rice also approached the president in the matter, mostly by letters, in which he shared Grey's position, stated with the greatest moderation yet yielding nothing. The Foreign Office rejected the second Lansing note as well, with Grey, through Spring Rice, saying to Wilson that Britain's position in restricting passage through its blockade was a must, "absolutely essential to our very existence." Faced with this intransigence, and Grey's way of arguing the point, the United States backed off, accepting the methods of the blockade as set forth in a new Order in Council. All things considered, the foreign secretary had handled the matter well, aided a great deal by his interlocutor at the embassy. Wilson took cognizance of this, writing to Spring Rice that United States accommodation to the blockade was due in part "to your fair spirit in these trying days."

The blockade and neutral rights issues would not go away, especially as American trade in the war zone continued to grow. For example in November 1914 Spring Rice reported copper shipped via the port of

New York had increased by 300 percent over the year previous and he referred to Denmark as "Germany's backdoor." Special interests had powerful friends in Congress and could be expected to protest to the State Department the sequestering of any American registered merchant ship. Spring Rice advised his chief in the matter by suggesting that every seizure be handled individually, on its own merits. Great Britain, according to its ambassador, must always appear to be working out arrangements to reduce friction with the United States. When the War Cabinet expressed its concern about the ease with which false manifests were obtained by ships leaving American ports Spring Rice made strong representations to Secretary of State Bryan and by insisting in moderate tones that procedures needed to be tightened he was able to get results. Various issues of commerce continued to vex Anglo-American diplomacy over the next two years with Spring Rice endeavoring to keep the atmosphere free of bitterness and recrimination, a practical approach to a thorny problem.

Neutrality. In neutral America Wilson's statement issued August 4, 1914, proclaimed a strict neutrality. (*See Document No. 23.*) But soon thereafter a vocal minority pro-Ally faction emerged and began to agitate for United States entry into the war. To them it was a war to defeat German militarism and/or to preserve the status quo, pre-1914. As the war progressed the clamor for involvement increased because of German violation of Belgian neutrality—"poor little Belgium"—the execution of Nurse Edith Cavell, the submarine campaign against commercial shipping, and finally the sinking of the *Lusitania* in May of 1915. British propaganda, for which the Germans appeared to provide enough fuel, was able to make a plausible cause for involvement. It was a movement President Wilson resolutely sought to stymie. England took heart from the demands of the interventionists, led by Theodore Roosevelt and supported by much of the eastern establishment, people TR had once referred to scornfully as Anglomaniacs. Regarding hopes of American involvement Spring Rice warned the War Cabinet time after time the United States under Wilson's leadership would never become an ally until in the president's judgment vital interests of the United States were at risk. The ambassador had been a student and observer of American society over the years; furthermore being in the country while the war was on gave him the opportunity to measure public opinion on a regular basis. He was not likely to be mistaken in his conclusion that, even after the loss of the *Lusitania*, the United States would remain aloof.

Wilson, the Peacemaker. There was still another consideration reenforcing the preference of Americans for peace, not war. President Wilson's deepest desire was to step in, at the right time, as a mediator, the apostle of peace amongst the warring nations. His trump card was American neutrality, a refusal to be drawn into the power struggle to aid one side or to help defeat the other. As long as he was true to that he preserved his chance to be an honest broker, a fair-minded opponent of war, the ultimate man of peace. This was his calling and he would be true to it. Whether the War Cabinet liked it or not there was to be no ready reversal of his peace objective. The dispatching of Colonel House on peace missions in 1915 and again in 1916 is clear evidence of this. Not to argue that Wilson would not have preferred to see the English and French prevail in a war to the death, but that western civilization could not afford to pay that high a price. "A peace at any price" leader was the taunt greeting Wilson by those who saw him as a coward. But neither disparagement nor sentiment could dissuade the president from his appointed task. Under these circumstances Spring Rice knew it was his duty to discourage his countrymen from believing America would soon to go war. Critics of his diplomacy in Whitehall and in the British press who denounced him as a do-nothing ambassador for being unable to persuade Wilson of the folly of standing aside as the world teetered on the brink of destruction betrayed their ignorance of America and its president. To sum up, Spring Rice was a trustworthy analyst of American public opinion, and a critical player in the efforts of the British government to keep friendly relations with United States as that nation pursued its own best interests. A further review of embassy diplomacy will show how this tactic succeeded and where it failed.

The Propaganda Issue. One of the issues Spring Rice had to deal with, a matter he considered beyond his duties as an accredited representative to a foreign government, was wartime propaganda. To a greater degree than ever before, a war for control of the popular mind became part of the reality of struggles between nations in the twentieth century, of which the Bryce Report is a clear example. (*See Document*

No. 24.) Spring Rice never denied the proposition but he fiercely resisted the idea that propaganda—information or disinformation—should emanate from his embassy. It was not simply a matter of "bad form." Fundamentally he rejected an assault on American public opinion as inconsistent with his conviction that people in a politically free society would be better left to making up their own minds on such grave issues as war or peace. He stressed again and again that American could not be hoodwinked into joining the Allies. At the end of the day he was to be proven right, yet in 1915 the end of the day was many months in the distance. Meanwhile the War Cabinet decided to set up an Office of Information under the direction of Sir Gilbert Parker. Parker proposed to be as blatantly propagandistic as the German ambassador, Johann Heinrich Count von Bernstorff had been when hostilities first broke out. Did British propaganda, so disdained by Spring Rice, have any tangible effect on President Wilson's conduct of diplomacy? Considering that as late as November 1916, Wilson was reelected to office having campaigned on the theme, "he kept us out of war," the whole exercise by Parker had problematical results. As Spring Rice wrote to A. J. Balfour who by that date had replaced Grey as foreign secretary, "It is doubtful we can change the weather by rigging the barometer." (*See Document No. 25.*) The accuracy of his judgment had already been borne out by American reaction to the sinking of the *Lusitania*. Wishful thinking in England when combined with ignorance of America promoted the view that the United States would certainly enter the war after so brutal an attack on defenseless people. But as Spring Rice warned: "It will take more than the *Lusitania*" to persuade the American president and people to go to war. (*See Document No. 26.*)

Lusitania Lost. The sinking of the *Lusitania* in May 1915 did have an impact on British-American diplomacy. Oddly enough it worked to aggravate rather than promote good will between Washington and London. Wilson's strong note of protest to the Kaiser denouncing the German U-boat attack produced a promise that in the future large passenger steamers would be spared destruction. Wilson believed he had thereby gained some German respect for neutral rights. As a man of peace he was easily persuaded that the pen was indeed mightier than the sword. America was pleased; Britain was deflated. In light of this concession the State Department took the position that London should also make concessions, easing the rules of blockade. The whole idea was rejected outright by the War Cabinet. Once again Spring Rice urged conciliation but conciliation had taken on the look of a failed policy in London. But was it? Take the issue of cotton as absolute contraband, meaning that it was no more protected from seizure than arms and ammunition. The American cotton states did not want their product on the contraband list. They preferred to allow cotton to sell freely on an open market. It was evident that a certain amount of United States grown cotton was slipping through the blockade, entering neutral ports for sale to the Germans. Spring Rice proposed to Colonel House that Britain purchase the entire American cotton crop at a fixed but attractive price per pound, but somewhat less than the 30 cents a pound the Germans said they were willing to pay. The proposal was a bold one which London was prepared to accept "in principle." In return for that agreement cotton was placed on the absolute contraband list. Conciliatory diplomacy was shown to continue to have a place in British-American relations, in war time as in peace time.

British Finances. One of the most serious problems for the British government was financing the war with the costs immense and growing daily. In 1915 the War Cabinet proposed to float a billion dollar bond issue, the securities to be sold on the United States market. Spring Rice doubted such a huge sum could be raised, and that for two reasons. Americans were simply not accustomed to invest in foreign issues; and as the outlook for British victory in the war was murky, there would be insufficient incentive to invest in the bonds even at an attractive 6 percent rate of interest. His warnings went unheeded and in the late summer of 1915 a team of experts led by Rufus Daniel Isaacs, Lord Reading arrived in New York. After consulting with a group of Wall Street bankers it was decided to reduce the size of the borrowing to $500 million, a 50 percent cut. Even so, after two months of trading only $370 million had been subscribed and of that but $33 million by private investors. The rest had been absorbed by brokers and investment bankers. Nonetheless there was a bright side to this mixture of success and failure, as the British viewed it. The economic ties binding the American economy to the British war effort had been fastened. About 40 percent of American exports depended on British war orders and the United States was awash in prosperity. Did this latter consideration provide London with a psychological bargaining chip? Perhaps it did. Whether the time was to come when a bargain was to be made would, as always, depend on the interaction of men and events.

Blockade/Blacklist. The issue of the blockade persisted all through 1916 and at times was about to rupture Anglo-American friendship. At least Spring Rice interpreted the signs that way. The stepped-up blockade was due to the ability of the Royal Navy, for the first time, to apply maximum force, and the determination of the new men in the cabinet to use this weapon to the limit, best summed up by Lloyd George's announced intention to "fight to the finish, a knock-out." The United States had accepted the fact of the blockade but always protested it in principle. But a tighter blockade with newer items on the absolute contraband list and the resort to the blacklist and the white list and interference with the mails caused outcries across the country. When his government rejected all formal protests Spring Rice warned of a growing hostility. "We are certainly invoking on our heads a great deal of indignation from a great many powerful people." Even British-born American officials complained HM government did not take the protests seriously enough. No aspect of British tactics was more fiercely resented than the blacklisting of American firms suspected of dealing with Germany through neutral countries. The secretary of state told Colonel House: "This blacklisting order of the English is causing tremendous irritation and we will have to do something." To the president it was the last straw and he set forth his arguments very clearly to Spring Rice. As he told House both Spring Rice and the French ambassador, Jean Jules Jusserand, think it "a stupid blunder." Wilson in consequence began to consider asking Congress to authorize him to restrict or to prohibit exportation to the Allies. Spring Rice cabled Grey, recounting the president's extreme displeasure. In seeking to moderate presidential anger the ambassador took a soft line suggesting to Grey each blacklisting case be treated as unique. Firms might also be allowed to request removal from the blacklist, and this should be done if the facts warranted it. Grey was willing to be reasonable in the face of such official American indignation, but he was opposed by some ranking foreign office staff. In this instance Spring Rice's advice prevailed, a good example of how much Sir Edward respected his opinion, at least in matters of detail. Yet it was the big picture that had motivated the advice.

By October 1916, the ambassador was fearful that England and France could not carry on the war much longer without significant additions of American credit. His message to Grey urging a relaxation of blacklisting was bluntly put: "If you are independent of the United States you can do what you like but if you have proclaimed your dependence, and that being so, you must pay the price." It was unpopular advice but Grey, following the line of the argument, recognized the wisdom of making concessions. Spring Rice reported back to his chief that Grey's attitude "gave great satisfaction." (*See Document No. 27.*)

House and Grey. Uncertain of reelection in the early months of 1916 Wilson was to launch another peace making attempt. Spring Rice interpreted the move this way. The president "is bent on peace. He is determined to give Germany its chance; his great ambition is to be the mediator of peace without victory, which would give the world permanent international law and mutual confidence." But once Wilson would come to realize that peace was not to be, he probably would no longer be willing to pay any price to avoid the menace of the submarine. This new peace initiative, the House-Grey Memorandum as it was termed, was centered in a request for the Allies and the Central Powers to state their war aims and their peace terms to end hostilities. Spring Rice hoped the British press would fall silent; he advised the Foreign Office to make no quick response. In London the cabinet considered the American proposal carefully, held back a reply for the purpose of further study and eventually supplied a sufficiently detailed statement of aims and terms to be encouraging, but made no commitment. For their part the Germans held aloof, as a consequence of which the peace plan failed. but the whole affair showed the British to be somewhat reasonable in sharp contrast to their enemy. (*See Document No. 28.*)

Sussex Pledge. One event promising well for Anglo-American cooperation was Germany's continued use of unrestricted submarine attacks on merchant shipping. This led to the sinking of the channel steamer *Sussex* in March of 1916. Wilson wrote a stern note of protest and warning, but it was something less than an ultimatum. To the surprise of many and to the dismay of the British who were hoping the sinking of the *Sussex* would lead to a sharp deterioration of German-American relations, Berlin responded to Wilson's protest by offering the

Sussex Pledge. Thereafter merchantmen would not be sunk without prior warning to facilitate evacuation of the ship. The Sussex Pledge amounted to a stunning diplomatic victory for the president and an unfulfilled opportunity for Britain. Spring Rice characterized the situation in the United States immediately after the sinking in a matter of fact way: "It can not be said the United States has been set on fire [by the sinking] and it can be said with certainty that if there is any sign of a conflagration every effort will be made to extinguish the flames." In fact, President Wilson had done exactly that, thereby preserving the opportunity, should the right time arrive, to step in and mediate the end of the war. (*See Document No. 29.*)

This diplomatic victory emboldened the president to preach peace without victory more vigorously, and it put a new complexion on the up-coming presidential campaign. Peace without victory was translated into "he kept us out of war" and when the election returns were in he had defeated Charles Evans Hughes to win a second term. The irony therefore is dramatic. Within a month of his swearing in Wilson went before Congress to ask for a declaration of war against Germany. Both men and events had conspired to wreck his peace agenda.

The Kaiser's 1917 decision to unleash the u-boats and renew unrestricted submarine warfare was a bitter pill for the president to swallow and he faced the unhappy task of choosing between war for his country and humiliation. As Spring Rice was to report: "the feeling is the country is gradually increasing in intensity owing to the effect of the German declaration of ruthless warfare . . . the sense that something has to be done to unify the nation and the people for war was growing." Once the sinkings began on February 1 war was only a matter of time. The ambassador, however, reported all this matter of factly, in keeping with his characteristic note of caution.

Zimmermann Telegram. Americans, and especially those living in the south and west, were furious when the Zimmermann Telegram was made public in March. The German proposal that Mexico join in a war against the United States with the prospects of regaining the American southwest dramatized the German threat to mainland United States. Spring Rice told of an almost panic reaction sweeping the nation and of his fear many innocent German-Americans might be victims of indiscriminate violence. Meanwhile American ships continued to be torpedoed, the sinking of the *Algonquin* in particular exciting public opinion. At long last events were moving in such a way as to realize the fulfillment of the long hoped for American entry into the war. British diplomacy had triumphed. As for Spring Rice he was summarily recalled in December 1917, and died on his way home. (*See Document No. 30.*)

CHAPTER 7

WARTIME DIPLOMACY— AMERICAN CONDUCT

Ambassadorial Profile. Walter Hines Page would have been a perfect envoy, or as close to perfection as one could imagine, had his ambassadorship spread across an era devoid of a major international conflict. But that was not to be. 1914–1918, years that formed the greater part of Page's time in London, saw the ambassador overwhelmed by the specter of the Great War. He pondered almost daily its meaning for western civilization. At the center of his worry was the fate of the English-speaking world, the far flung British Empire and the United States with its territorial possessions. As the American spokesman he had the duty of presenting his government's reactions to the war and the policies it sought to pursue in consequence. For him this would not be an easy task to carry out. Great Britain, he was convinced, was fighting for survival and therefore was bound to fight the war with survival as paramount, irrespective of how this would or would not impact on the United States. Like the British, Page was personally committed to victory over Germany so that the question arises almost at once: could Page favor American neutrality and British victory at one and the same time? What might be expected of an ambassador who, duty bound, was to read a dispatch from his government critical of London policy, and then say to the foreign secretary: "I do not agree with this; let us consider how we shall answer it." The diplomacy of Woodrow Wilson had a twofold purpose: to look after American rights on the high seas and to remain neutral until such time as American interests were at grave risk. In all candor it was not a policy Ambassador Page could endorse. Wilson's diplomacy was often poorly served as a result.

As has been often stated in explanation if not in defense of Page's attitude, his highest policy objective was that of Anglo-American cooperation. He was quite literally obsessed with the notion. If only Great Britain and the United States were to stand together, so his thinking ran, the future belonged to them and to them alone. As he once stated: "if there were the tightest sort of alliance between Great Britain and the United States . . . anything we'd say would go." In as much as "the tightest sort of alliance" did not exist Page was likely to have insufficient confidence in and therefore little enthusiasm for making forceful representations of Wilson's diplomacy. A good example of what can only be called a conflict of interest on the ambassador's part occurred over the Washington proposal for all belligerents to observe the provisions of the Declaration of London. It has been shown how Spring Rice protested against this as he fought his country's diplomatic battle in Washington. London was adamant in its rejection of the idea, but no more so than the State Department was adamant in insisting upon it. Wilson and Lansing, at the time a counsellor at state, directed Page to "talk tough" with the British. Instead he cabled a dispatch to Washington in which he took a hardline against his own government's position. The president became directly involved as he cautioned Page: "Beg that you will not regard the position of this government as merely academic," whereupon he noted that his ambassador was out of touch with opinion back home. Page was exasperated enough to contemplate handing in his resignation. The issue was only settled when the United States withdrew its demand for compliance with the Declaration of London. It is of some interest to contrast Wilson's evaluation of Spring Rice's role with that of Page. He wrote the British ambassador as previously stated complimenting him on his "fair spirit in trying times." About the same time Wilson told Colonel House of the danger to his policies possibly arising from the intense feeling Page had for the British cause. One important effect of all this was the Wilson–Page relationship, once marked by mutual admiration and trust, virtually fell apart.

Page Loses Influence. Further evidence of this breakdown may be seen when Colonel House came to London in February 1915, on his first peace mission. Page greeted him warmly and the two had several long, serious conversations about the progress of the war, the issues dividing nations, and the hopes for peace. House also met privately with Sir Edward Grey, visiting him at his private residence rather than in Whitehall. Page remained ignorant of this and apparently did not realize the president no longer wanted him to handle all exchanges between him and the foreign secretary because of his extreme Anglophilia. The fact is Page's popularity with officials in London disqualified him to represent his country as Washington wanted him to do. Something similar befell Spring Rice, but in Page's case it was much more clear cut. For example, House suggested to Grey that they deal with all important matters through a private code, to which only they would have access. The result was neither embassy was to have knowledge of the existence of the code or the contents of the messages thereby transmitted. The irony was London did not believe Spring Rice was doing enough to bring the United States into the war and Washington concluded Page was doing too much to try to achieve the same result.

The sinking of the *Lusitania* made a complete convert of Walter Hines Page to the cause of American entry into the war. He argued his position vehemently, beginning with his dispatches to the State Department the very day after the tragedy. If President Wilson wanted to be a peacemaker this was the ideal time for the United Sates to throw its weight into the military balance, in Page's judgment. He believed a settlement to Anglo-American advantage would quickly follow. Not to go to war, furthermore, would cause his nation to lose all respect, even among those in England most kindly disposed toward America. From being privately pro-British Page now went public. According to one leading authority the loss of the *Lusitania* "brought out the worst in Page as an ambassador." What exactly does this mean? In the larger sense Page might just as well have considered himself to be ambassador from London rather than to London, so pronounced were his views. More specifically, from May 1915 down to April 1917, when war came to America Wilson was striving mightily to keep the nation uncommitted while Page was straining every diplomatic muscle to get his country to make a commitment. To say that president and ambassador were working at cross purposes is hardly deniable. Page did have a strong card to play, at least hypothetically. The hypothesis went this way: if Wilson wanted to influence the peace, he could do so only by reason of the participation by the United States in the war on land and on sea. Then and only then could Wilson realistically expect to be seated at a peace conference, once hostilities were over. For Page everything seemed to stem from the assault on the *Lusitania*, which to him was an attack on civilization and one deserving of condign punishment. And only the United States could bring this about, and then, only by war on Germany. Using 20/20 hindsight Page was correct in his reasoning, but this is not often a fair gauge with which to measure decisions. Besides, Wilson bore the ultimate responsibility, and not his old-time friend, for leading the nation into war and he was most reluctant to do so.

Last Days of an Ambassador. The diplomatic weather was to change. Once again it was a combination of men and events, the Kaiser ordering a resumption of unrestricted submarine war, to take effect February 1. But there was more, as has been noted. Conceding the entry of the United States into the war the Kaiser was prepared to lure Mexico into an alliance by promising the return of Texas, New Mexico, and Arizona to Mexico should Germany prevail. As stated in the Zimmermann telegram it proved to be a bold but utterly foolish move. Wilson would now have to put his campaign for peace without victory aside. Diplomatic relations were broken between Washington and Berlin, February 3. From that day down to April 2, when the president addressed the Congress to acknowledge a state of war existed between the two powers the world of Anglo-American affairs changed dramatically, as did the mind and spirit of Walter Hines Page. Even as Wilson proceeded cautiously toward a full scale war the ambassador believed his mission had been achieved. But the president was somewhat slow of foot, preparing only to arm American cargo ships. Anti-interventionist elements in Congress saw this for what it was, a step toward a formal declaration of war, and filibustered the proposed legislation, only to have Wilson legalize his proposal by invoking a law dating from 1797. In the logical order arming the merchantmen was bound to create shooting incidents leading to a de facto armed conflict. Page was impatient with his chief, very probably because he had been waiting for so long to witness a full and formal American commitment.

Meanwhile on his own initiative Page canvassed various departments of his host government, trying to learn just where American help was most urgently needed. Such high-level efforts could pay off once Congress responded to Wilson's call for war, which came April 4, two days after the president announced that a state of war existed. At long last the Yanks were coming. All of which was to alter the diplomatic game and Page's place in it. (*See Document No. 31.*) But less so than was the situation with Spring Rice in Washington; after all Page was never removed as ambassador while the war was on. The American's role and responsibilities had changed drastically, nonetheless, once the United States was fully in the fight. Economic and military matters called for specialized knowledge and expertise beyond Page's capability as relations between London and Washington took on a different and more concentrated focus. By September, he believed his job at the embassy was "really done" and he was correct in his judgment.

CHAPTER 8

RESOLUTION AND CONCLUSION

Synopsis of Anglo-American Diplomacy. As an analysis of the embassy work of Spring Rice and Page has clearly shown diplomacy need not and was not confined to the accustomed peacetime channels. Whether the perspective is from London or from Washington there is notable, and it might be said convincing, evidence to support the conclusion calling for a thematic/synthetic resolution of the wartime relations between Britain and America. One such theme is public opinion as expressed through the press or through the activities of interest groups. Another is the leadership required by the exigencies of total war. A third is the function of ancillary officials, who may or may not be of high rank but who are answerable to a final authority. The place of the intelligence services should not be overlooked, as clandestine as that might be. Finally it is appropriate to offer an assessment of the full range of Anglo-American diplomacy as it influenced the realities of the years 1914–1917. In like vein it can be useful to give a verdict on the meaning of the Anglo-American rapprochement from 1895 to 1917, the birthing years of the special relationship.

Public Opinion Counts. When it comes to public opinion the contrast between England and America is striking, a difference that goes a long way in explaining and justifying the strains put on the integrity of both peoples. The British populace was united from the outset of the war, as were the French and Germans for that matter. Such was magnetic power of nationalism. "For King and Country" was no idle phrase, it expressed the yearnings of the people, taken down to the tap root. "My country right or wrong but my country" was a conviction reenforced by the certainty that Germany had started the war, that it had violated Belgium neutrality which it had solemnly swore to observe in order to get the jump on France, Britain's ally. Looking at the immediate causes of the war, including the Kaiser's blank cheque to Austria-Hungary to destroy Serbia as distinct from its remote origins, it was easy enough for the British to unite in their struggle for survival. America was different. It was a polyglot nation where mastery of English was the ticket to advancement but a ticket not universally enjoyed. There were two large segments of the population by their very nature anti-British: German-Americans and Irish-Americans. Theodore Roosevelt may well have railed against "hyphenated-Americans" but they were nevertheless a fact of American society. British propaganda represented the Germans as "the Huns" and as such, barbarians, something bound to give offense to millions of German-Americans, native born and naturalized. Irish-Americans had no love for their oppressors in the old country nor were they in any way reassured the British had changed as witnessed in their response to the Easter Week uprising of 1916 and the execution of the Irish hero, Roger Casement, despite a Senatorial resolution protesting his death sentence. Therefore as a nation American public opinion ranged from indifference to the outcome of the war to the full-throated demand of interventionists to join the Allies in a moral crusade. Opinion in the United States vacillated with the fortunes of war but even the more advanced pro-British elements had difficulty accepting the black list and interference with mails. Wilson's policy of strict neutrality derived from a variety of considerations, one of which was the diversity of the national origins of the American citizenry *ca.* 1914.

Leadership Is Vital. Because there was no immediate identity of wartime interests by Great Britain and the United States the role of the chief executive differed one from the other. The responsibility of the prime minister, working through his cabinet was to bring together the numerous factors—economic, financial, naval, military, diplomatic and psychological—in such a way as to win the war. Asquith lacked the dynamism of purpose and personality to bring it off. Lloyd George however was amply supplied with vitality and determination, if only out of desperation, to galvanize the nation. He exuded the confidence essential to convince the people, high and low, the day of victory was attainable, despite the darkness of the hour. It was easier for the prime minister to know what had to be done to save his country from disaster than it was for the American president to sell neutrality to all his countrymen. Neither Asquith nor Lloyd George need worry about a disloyal opposition, whereas Wilson could hardly ignore the demands of the irrepressible Theodore Roosevelt to go to war. Not that neutrality lacked a powerful appeal: no casualty lists, satisfaction in taking the high moral ground of peace without victory, or more cynically, why fight England's war? It is only being realistic to appreciate Wilson's neutrality policy as he faced the challenge of reelection in 1916, a year when the carnage on the Western Front had reached, if not surpassed, an awesome level. For all his sentimental attachment to things English, Wilson proved himself a true American statesman, not an Anglo-American statesman. And he suffered real abuse from the pro-interventionists in consequence.

Indispensable Personnel. The evidence is ample the chief executives relied to a large extent on a variety of subordinates in carrying out their policies. Here the American system of government, a centralized executive authority, was better suited to decision making that the cabinet system. Asquith in particular had to assemble a coalition cabinet, hardly able to ignore the conservative party irrespective of how united the nation was in fighting the war. As foreign secretaries both Grey and Balfour were strong minded men better able than Asquith and perhaps no less able than Lloyd George in keeping foreign policy in their charge. On the American side Secretary of State Bryan exited after less than a year of war and his successor, Lansing, had portfolio without real power. As called for in the constitution and established by precedent the president was, and virtually had to be, his own secretary of state. Lincoln had clearly shown the way in this regard. True, Wilson made use of Colonel House, and that is exactly what he did, he used House as the occasion arose. Occasionally House might seem to taken an initiative of his own but he was always directly answerable to the president; he knew it and Wilson knew it and House acted accordingly. The work of the intelligence services in the conduct of diplomacy, no less than in the conduct of war, can not be ignored. British intelligence, especially in the activities of Captain William Hall of Naval Intelligence and of Captain William Wiseman of M. I.6, must be taken into account. Hall was the man who broke the German codes. He knew before anyone else in London or Washington the content of the Zimmermann note, and he took it upon himself to release the information at the time most opportune for influencing American public opinion against Germany. British naval intelligence also tapped the communication lines of the American embassy allowing the War Cabinet to be privy to the exchanges between Ambassador Page and the State Department. As for Wiseman he became the confidant of Colonel House in December 1916. For the next several weeks, down to April 1917, a critical period as the United States edged toward war, Wiseman, via House, had an insider's knowledge of the drift of things, sharing it, of course, with his government. Because of House's deliberate effort to circumvent the embassies Spring Rice and Page became superfluous as the diplomatic drama reached a climax. The Colonel put great faith in Wiseman's appraisal of Anglo-American relations at the time and made use of the captain's direct contacts with key ministers. He was able to convince President Wilson of the value of Wiseman's good offices and that strengthened his hand in dealings both with Washington and London. Yet it must be said in a resolution of the question regarding the locus of diplomatic responsibility the two embassies proved themselves indispensable to their respective governments. It was their everyday conduct of affairs that, in the last analysis, helped to bring the nations together after a long period of misunderstanding and distrust. That was no small accomplishment.

Rapprochement Decides the War. Only a score of years separated the Venezuelan boundary dispute from the sinking of the *Lusitania*. In that relatively short time as the history of nations is measured the old hostility between England and America had been replaced by cordiality and a consciousness of the historic potential created by the cooperation of the two English speaking polities. It is not too much to claim that save for the rapprochement the 1914 war would have ended with an outcome gravely different from historical fact, and one not advantageous to the British empire. If it is idle to speculate in this way in detail it is nonetheless realistic to contend the world of the twentieth century would be a different place had Germany avoided outright defeat. Think what you will about United States entry into the conflict as "last minute johnnies." The nearness of Great Britain to financial collapse as it faced the summer campaigning season of 1917 would have become total collapse save for American intervention. The United States was a *deus ex machina* salvaging Britain's war effort carried out at such a staggering cost to itself. Wartime diplomacy taken all in all had brought about the desired effect.

In the Long View. The Anglo-American rapprochement is one of the epochal diplomatic events in modern history. In its mature stage of evolution it became a "spiritual relationship," an association so intimate that it has had no equivalent in the history of sovereign nations. To be sure it was more than a diplomatic affair, grounded as it was on a common language and literature, a common bond of law and government, and a common public philosophy celebrating the rights of the individual over and against the state. It proved to be a bulwark thrown up to counter the revolution of nihilism of the succeeding generation, a philosophy of life that combined treacherously with an inherited nationalism to bring about an even greater war. The special relationship endured and the values upon it rested endured as well.

PART II

DOCUMENTS

DOCUMENT NO. 1

RICHARD OLNEY ON VENEZUELA
AND THE U.S. FIAT IN THE WESTERN
HEMISPHERE, 1895*

*This Note represents not simply an expanded statement of the Monroe
Doctrine but virtually its rebirth. The Doctrine had lain fallow for many
decades, surfacing only occasionally and then voiced in somewhat muted
tones. Now it was fully resurrected and the message of warning was loud and
clear: the United States was sovereign and was prepared to contest any failure to recognize it.*

γ　　　　　　γ　　　　　　γ

That America is in no part open to colonization, though the proposition
was not universally admitted at the time of its first enunciation [in
1823], has long been universally conceded. We are now concerned,
therefore, only with that other practical application of the Monroe doctrine the disregard of which by an European power is to be deemed an
act of unfriendliness towards the United States. The precise scope and
limitations of this rule cannot be too clearly apprehended. It does not
establish any general protectorate by the United States over other
American states. It does not relieve any American state from its obligations as fixed by international law nor prevent any European power directly interested from enforcing such obligations or from inflicting mer-
ited punishment for the breach of them. It does not contemplate any
interference in the internal affairs of any American state or in the relations between it and other American states. It does not justify any attempt on our part to change the established form of government of any
American state or to prevent the people of such state from altering that
form according to their own will and pleasure. The rule in question has
but a single purpose and object. It is that no European power or combination of European powers shall forcibly deprive an American state of
the right and power of self-government and of shaping for itself its own
political fortunes and destinies. . . .

Today the United States is practically sovereign on this continent,

* *Foreign Relations* (1895), I, p. 558.

and its fiat is law upon the subjects to which it confines its interposition. Why? It is not because of the pure friendship or good will felt for it. It is not simply by reason of its high character as a civilized state, nor because wisdom and justice and equity are the invariable characteristics of the dealings of the United States. It is because, in addition to all other grounds, its infinite resources combined with its isolated position render it master of the situation and practically invulnerable as against any or all other powers.

Thus, as already intimated, the British demand that her right to a portion of the disputed territory shall be acknowledged before she will consent to an arbitration as to the rest seems to stand upon nothing but her own *ipse dixit*. She says to Venezuela, in substance: "You can get none of the debatable land by force, because you are not strong enough; you can get none by a treaty, because I will not agree; and you can take your chance of getting a portion by arbitration, only if you first agree to abandon to me such other portion as I may designate." It is not perceived how such an attitude can be defended nor how it is reconcilable with that love of justice and fair play so eminently characteristic of the English race. It in effect deprives Venezuela of her free agency and puts her under virtual duress. Territory acquired by reason of it will be as much wrested from her by the strong hand as if occupied by British troops or covered by British fleets. It seems therefore quite impossible that this position of Great Britain should be assented to by the United States, or that, if such position be adhered to with the result of enlarging the bounds of British Guiana, it should not be regarded as amounting, in substance, to an invasion and conquest of Venezuelan territory.

DOCUMENT NO. 2

WILLIAM L. SCRUGGS ON
"BRITISH AGGRESSION IN VENEZUELA"*

Scruggs' inflammatory pamphlet was an important contribution to the war of words emanating from the boundary dispute. It is an easy matter to question the motivation of Scruggs but it is much harder to disagree with the argument set forth. It is also evident from what he wrote that he felt his readers and especially his friends in the Congress, might require a great deal of education in the realities of Latin America, its present condition, and its future importance to American policy in the hemisphere. Referring to the long standing efforts of Britain to dominate Latin American trade, dating from the Asiento (1714) Scruggs came directly to the point.

γ   γ   γ

These facts carry their own comment. Studies in connection with any good map of the country, they have a startling significance. The South American continent, by its peculiar configuration, is naturally divided into three immense valleys—the Orinoco, the Amazon, and the Plata. Each of the valleys is, in itself, a complete network of fluviatile navigation, open from the sea to the remote interior. Those of the Guayaquil, Atrato, and Magdalena are of but little consequence in comparison; for the chain of the Andes, extending from Patagonia along the Pacific, and thence eastward along the Caribbean to the Gulf of Paria, constitute a natural barrier to the interior. But there are no mountain chains traversing the continent from east to west; no such barriers to communication between the valleys of the Orinoco, Amazon, and Plata; and those three great rivers communicate by distinct bifurcations. Hence, the dominion of the mouth of either by such a power as England, would, in the course of time, and almost as a natural consequence, open the way to pretensions over the others . . . .

Let it be borne in mind also that the country which is being thus ruthlessly despoiled of its territorial sovereignty is not in some remote and inaccessible corner of the earth with which we neither have, nor hope to have, any very direct political or commercial relations. It is near-

* William L. Scruggs, *British Aggression in Venezuela* (Atlanta, Ga.: Franklin Printing Company, 1895) pp. 14–15, 24–25.

est of all our South American neighbors. Its political capital, one of the most beautiful and attractive on the continent, is less then six days' journey from Washington. Its commercial marts, second to none on the Caribbean shores, are directly opposite to ours on the South Atlantic and Gulf coasts, and distant less then five days' sail. Even the harbors and inlets of Guayana and the Orinoco delta are only about five days' sail from New York. It is the only South American republic with which we are in direct and regular weekly communication by an American line of steamships. Its people are among the most intelligent and progressive of all Latin America. And our commerce with it is now about double, in volume and value, our trade with any of the other trans-Caribbean free States. These conditions alone, even if others were wanting, could hardly fail to inspire our sympathy and enlist our active interposition.

DOCUMENT NO. 3

JOSEPH CHAMBERLAIN PREACHES ANGLO-AMERICAN ACCORD*

One of the most influential members of Liberal Party leadership in the 1890s, Joseph Chamberlain was fully committed to the idea of Anglo-American solidarity, politically and commercially. His Birmingham Town Hall speech is eloquent evidence of this. What is no less significant was the way his proposals were received. It is not a matter of preaching to be saved, but of converting the doubters to embrace the cause of Anglo-American friendship. Clearly he was prepared to spare no effort.

γ　　　　　　　γ　　　　　　　γ

Now the first point that I want to impress upon you is this. It is the crux of the situation. Since the Crimean War, nearly 50 years ago, the policy of this country has been a policy of strict isolation. We have had no allies—I am afraid we have had no friends. (Laughter.) That is not due altogether to the envy which is undoubtedly felt at our success; it is due in part to the suspicion that we are acting in our own selfish interests, and were willing that other people should draw the chestnuts out of the fire for us: that we would take no responsibilities, whilst we were glad enough to profit by the work of others. In this way we have avoided entangling alliances, we have escaped many dangers; but we must accept the disadvantages that go with such a policy. As long as the other Great Powers of Europe were also working for their own hand, and were separately engaged, I think the policy we have pursued—consistently pursued—was undoubtedly the right policy for this country. (Hear, hear.) It was better we should preserve our liberty of action than become mixed up with quarrels with which possibly we had no concern. (Hear, hear.) But now in recent years a different complexion has been placed upon the matter. A new situation has arisen, and it is right the people of this country should have it under their consideration. All the powerful States of Europe have made alliances, and as long as we keep outside these alliances, as long as we are envied by all, and suspected by all, and as long as we have interests which at one time or another conflict with the interests of all, we are liable to be confronted at any moment with a

* *The Times*, May 1, 1895.

combination of Great Powers so powerful that not even the most extreme, the most hotheaded politician would be able to contemplate it without a certain sense of uneasiness. (Hear, hear.) That is the situation which I want you to have in view, which you must always have in view, when you are considering the results of the foreign policy of any Government in this country. We stand alone, and we may be confronted with such a combination as that I have indicated to you. What is the first duty of a Government under these circumstances? I say, without hesitation, that the first duty is to draw all parts of the Empire closer together (loud and prolonged cheers) fo infuse into them a spirit of united and of Imperial patriotism. (Cheers.) We have not neglected that primary duty. (Cheers.) We have pursued it steadfastly and with results that are patent to all the world. Never before in the history of the British Empire have the ties which connected us with our great colonies and dependencies been stronger, never before has the sense of common interests in trade and in defence and in war, never before has the sense of these interests been more strongly felt or more cordially expressed. (Cheers.)

What is our next duty? It is to establish and to maintain bonds of permanent amity with our kinsmen across the Atlantic. (Loud cheers.) They are a powerful and a generous nation. They speak our language, they are bred of our race. (Loud cheers.) Their laws, their literature, their standpoint upon every question are the same as ours; their feeling, their interest in the cause of humanity and the peaceful development of the world are identical with ours. (Cheers.) I do not know what the future has in store for us. I do not know what arrangements may be possible with us, but this I know and feel—that the closer, the more cordial, the fuller and the more definite these arrangements are, with the consent of both peoples, the better it will be for both and for the world. (Loud cheers.) And I even go so far as to say that, terrible as war may be, even war itself would be cheaply purchased if in a great and noble cause the Stars and Stripes and the Union Jack should wave together (Loud and prolonged cheers) over an Anglo–Saxon alliance. Now, it is one of the most satisfactory results of Lord Salisbury's policy (Cheers) that at the present time these two great nations understand each other better than they have ever done since more than a century ago. (Hear, hear.) They were separated by the blunder of the British Government.

DOCUMENT NO. 4

THE JAMESON RAID AS
REPORTED IN *THE TIMES* *

The Jameson Raid was an act of undisguised provocation by irregular British forces against the farmers of the Transvaal and the Orange Free State. It very nearly caused a war between Great Britain and Imperial Germany; at the very least it sowed bitterness and suspicion between the two powers. The United States government sought to pursue a policy of neutrality toward the nations in question, but by 1895, the year the raid took place, pro-British sentiment in America could be sensed. Relations between the Boers and the British continued on a collision course, leading on to the Boer War.

γ   γ   γ

The Transvaal. A telegram from Sir Hercules Robinson, dated 7 January, was received yesterday at the Colonial Office, stating that Johannesburg had surrendered unconditionally, and that the arms were given up. President Kruger had intimated his intention of handing over Dr Jameson and the other prisoners to the High Commissioner on the borders of Natal. The British government might therefore feel satisfied that the crisis is over, and that all danger of further hostilities is at an end. — A Pretoria telegram of Monday describes the arrival of the High Commissioner there, and says a most bitter anti-British feeling prevails among the burghers, who are only held in check by the powerful personal influence of the president. They angrily resent the necessity for leaving their farms and occupations, and demand a speedy and final settlement and the full possession of their country under one undisputed rule. The whole of the Transvaal and Orange Free State Boers are under arms, the latter being massed on the frontier, awaiting the course of events. — Despatches from Cape Town indicate that in Cape Colony and Rhodesia there is a strong feeling of indignation against the National Union agitators at Johannesburg for having deserted and betrayed Dr Jameson. Meetings have been held and resolutions carried expressing regret at the position in which Dr Jameson and his comrades are placed and recognising the courage and endurance they displayed. —

* *The Times*, January 10, 1896.

Our correspondent at Johannesburg, telegraphing under date 2 January *via* Bloemfontein, sends some interesting further details respecting the final fight at Valkfontein and Dr Jameson's surrender, of which he was an eye-witness. The Boers, he says, spoke in feeling terms of the splendid bravery shown by their assailants. — According to a Krugersdorp despatch, Dr Jameson's surrender was unconditional. He narrowly escaped being shot in the market square of Krugersdorp by the incensed Boers, but was saved by the commandant, who threatened to shoot the first man who raised his rifle. — In Cape Town the general feeling on Monday was one of anxiety regarding the ultimate issue of the crisis. On Tuesday it was reported there that the Transvaal government demanded the banishment of Mr Rhodes and Dr Jameson from Africa, and an enormous fine from the Chartered Company as an indemnity for the violation by its forces of the territory of the republic . . . .

DOCUMENT NO. 5

THE MISSION OF THE ANGLO-SAXON RACE, ACCORDING TO JOSIAH STRONG*

As early as 1885, the year Strong published Our Country, *from which the following excerpt is taken, there were pronounced suppositions of the superiority of Anglo-Saxon nations, more specifically Great Britain and her dominions and the United States. In other words the feeling that the two English-speaking peoples should unite in purpose was part of the* zeitgeist *some years before the American republic became an imperialist power. A clergyman, Strong was utterly convinced of his thesis and therefore was intent on convincing others of the right of his race to rule. Because Strong's argument may sound hopelessly out of date this excerpt should be read in conjunction with the following Document No. 6.*

γ   γ   γ

Every race which has deeply impressed itself on the human family has been the representative of some great idea—one or more—which has given direction to the nation's life and form to its civilization. Among the Egyptians this seminal idea was life, among the Persians it was light, among the Hebrews it was purity, among the Greeks it was beauty, among the Romans it was law. The Anglo-Saxon is the representative of two great ideas, which are closely related. One of them is that of civil liberty. Nearly all of the civil liberty in the world is enjoyed by Anglo-Saxons: the English, the British colonists, and the people of the United States. To some, like to Swiss, it is permitted by the sufferance of their neighbors; others, like the French, have experimented with it; but, in modern times, the peoples whose love of liberty has won it, and whose genius for self-government has preserved it, have been Anglo-Saxons. The noblest races have always been lovers of liberty. That love ran strong in early German blood, and has profoundly influenced the institutions of all the branches of the great German family; but it was left for the Anglo-Saxon branch fully to recognize the right of the individual to himself, and formally to declare it the foundation stone of government.

The other great idea of which the Anglo-Saxon is the exponent is that of a pure spiritual Christianity. It was no accident that the great refor-

* *Our Country* (New York: Baker and Taylor Company, 1891), pp. 200-201.

95

mation of the sixteenth century originated among a Teutonic, rather than a Latin people. It was the fire of liberty burning in the Saxon heart that flamed up against the absolutism of the Pope. Speaking roughly, the peoples of Europe which are Celtic are Catholic, and those which are Teutonic are Protestant; and where the Teutonic race was purest, there Protestantism spread with the greatest rapidity. But, with rare and beautiful exceptions, Protestantism on the continent has degenerated into mere formalism. By confirmation at a certain age, the state churches are filled with members who generally know nothing of a personal spiritual experience. In obedience to a military order, a regiment of German soldiers files into church and partakes of the sacrament, just as it would shoulder arms or obey any other word of command. It is said that, in Berlin and Leipsic, only a little over one per cent. of the Protestant population are found in church. Protestantism on the continent seems to be about as poor in spiritual life and power as Catholicism. That means that most of the spiritual Christianity in the world is found among Anglo-Saxons and their converts; for this is the great missionary race. If we take all of the German missionary societies together, we find that, in the number of workers and amount of contributions, they do not equal the smallest of the three great English missionary societies. The year that Congregationalists in the United States gave one dollar and thirty-seven cents per caput to foreign missions, the members of the great German State Church gave only three-quarters of a cent per caput to the same cause. Evidently it is chiefly to the English and the American peoples that we must look for the evangelization of the world.

DOCUMENT NO. 6

ALBERT J. BEVERIDGE'S
"ON THE MISSION OF OUR RACE"*

Fifteen years after Josiah Strong sang his paean of praise for the Anglo-Saxon race the American senator, Albert J. Beveridge, echoed his sentiments in a speech on the Senate floor. Beveridge had called for the American Establishment to glory in its calling; Beveridge addressed the nation and in so doing sought to win high and to embrace the mission of uplifting the "lesser breeds without law." He was one of the most vocal defenders of economic imperialism and colonial expansion which was for him a commercial opportunity and the duty of the American nation.

γ γ γ

Mr. President, the times call for candor. The Philippines are ours forever, "territory belonging to the United States," as the Constitution calls them. And just beyond the Philippines are China's illimitable markets. We will not retreat from either. We will not repudiate our duty in the archipelago. We will not abandon our opportunity in the Orient. We will not renounce our part in the mission of our race, trustee, under God, of the civilization of the world. And we will move forward to our work, not howling out regrets like slaves whipped to their burdens, but with gratitude for a task worthy of our strength, and thanksgiving to Almighty God that He has marked us as His chosen people, henceforth to lead in the regeneration of the world . . . .

Mr. President, this question is deeper than any question of party politics; deeper than any question of the isolated policy of our country even; deeper even than any question of constitutional power. It is elemental. It is racial. God has not been preparing the English-speaking and Teutonic peoples for a thousand years for nothing but vain and idle self-contemplation and self-admiration. No! He has made us the master organizers of the world to establish system where chaos reigns. He has given us the spirit of progress to overwhelm the forces of reaction throughout the earth. He has made us adepts in government that we may administer government among savage and senile peoples. Were it not for such a force as this the world would relapse into barbarism and

* *Congressional Record*, 56th Congress, 1st Session, 1899–1900, pt. I, pp. 704–712.

97

night. And of all our race He has marked the American people as His chosen nation to finally lead in the regeneration of the world. This is the divine mission of America, and it holds for us all the profit, all the glory, all the happiness possible to man. We are trustees of the world's progress, guardians of its righteous peace. The judgment of the Master is upon us: "Ye have been faithful over a few things; I will make you ruler over many things."

What shall history say of us? Shall it say that we renounced that holy trust, left the savage to his base condition, the wilderness to the reign of waste, deserted duty, abandoned glory, forget our sordid profit even, because we feared our strength and read the charter of our powers with the doubter's eye and and quibbler's mind? Shall it say that, called by events to captain and command the proudest, ablest, purest race of history in history's noblest work, we declined that great commission? Our fathers would not have had it so. No! They founded no paralytic government, incapable of the simplest acts of administration. They planted no sluggard people, passive while the world's work calls them. They established no reactionary nation. They unfurled no retreating flag.

That flag has never paused in its onward march. Who dares halt it now—now, when history's largest events are carrying it forward; now, when we are at last one people, strong enough for any task, great enough for any glory destiny can bestow? How comes it that our first century closes with the process of consolidating the American people into a unit just accomplished, and quick upon the stroke of that great hour presses upon us our world opportunity, world duty, and world glory, which none but a people welded into an indivisible nation can achieve or perform?

DOCUMENT NO. 7

THEODORE ROOSEVELT'S PRIVATELY EXPRESSED VIEWS ON THE BOER WAR*

The outbreak of the Boer War in 1899 placed American policy on the horns of a dilemma. Admired as underdogs by many Americans, could sentiment or even a thirst for justice be allowed to dictate the official policy of the United States toward the conflict? While still governor of the state of New York, Roosevelt took it upon himself to indicate in a private letter what his position was. Given the fact he would be in the White House from September 1901 to the end of the war, United States policy would be one of pro-British neutrality.

γ   γ   γ

The British behaved so well to us during the Spanish War that I have no patience with these people who keep howling against them. I was mighty glad to see them conquer the Mahdi for the same reason that I think we should conquer Aguinaldo. The Sudan and Matabeleland will be better off under England's rule, just as the Philippines will be under our rule. But as against the Boers, I think the policy of Rhodes and Chamberlain has been one huge blunder, and exactly as you say, the British have won only by crushing superiority in numbers where they have won at all. Generally they have been completely out-fought, while some of their blunders have been simply stupendous. Now of course I think it would be a great deal better if all the white people of South Africa spoke English, and if my Dutch kinsfolk over there grew to accept English as their language just as my people and I here have done, they would be a great deal better off. The more I have looked into this Boer War the more uncomfortable I have felt about it. Of course, this is for your eyes only. I do not want to mix in things which do not concern me, and I have no patience with the Senators and Representatives that attend anti-British meetings and howl about England. I notice that they are generally men that sympathized with Spain two years ago.

---

* Roosevelt to William Sewell, November 24, 1900, Roosevelt *Papers*.

DOCUMENT NO. 8

PARTICULARS OF THE
CLAYTON-BULWER TREATY (1850)*

More than fifty years after the signing of this convention its terms came to be a stumbling block both to American ambitions to build and fortify a canal and to the growing amity between the United States and Great Britain. As treaties go, it was a moderately lengthy statement of understanding, divided into seven articles. Certain of its provisions had become obsolete by developments across five decades, such as to give support and encouragement to such persons or companies as might undertake the construction (Art. VII). However it was Art. I that caused difficulty, and regarding which the British were made to give way. This article is given in its entirety.

γ   γ   γ

The Government of Great Britain and The United States hereby declare that neither the one nor the other will ever obtain or maintain for itself any exclusive controul over the said ship-canal; agreeing that neither will ever erect or maintain any fortifications commanding the same, or in the vicinity thereof, or occupy, or fortify, or colonize, or assume or exercise any dominion over Nicaragua, Costa Rica, the Mosquito Coast, or any part of Central America; nor will either make use of any protection which either affords, or may afford, or any alliance which either has, or may have, to or with any State or people, for the purpose of erecting or maintaining any such fortifications, or of occupying, fortifying, or colonizing Nicaragua, Costa Rica, the Mosquito Coast, or any part of Central America, or of assuming or exercising dominion over the same. Nor will Great Britain or The United States take advantage of any intimacy, or use any alliance, connection, or influence that either may possess with any State or Government through whose territory the said canal may pass, for the purpose of acquiring or holding, directly or indirectly, for the subjects or citizens of the one, any rights or advantages in regard to commerce or navigation through the said canal, which shall not be offered, on the same terms, to the subjects or citizens of the other.

* *Treaties*, Miller, David Hunter, ed. (Washington, D.C.: Government Printing Office, 1937) V, 672–3.

DOCUMENT NO. 9

WILLIAM MCKINLEY'S
IMPERIALIST GOSPEL*

In his annual message to congress in December 1898, President McKinley spoke softly about the need to move forward on building an interoceanic canal. His measured remarks belied the imperialist spirit that seems to have begun to possess him. The very next year, 1899, in a public statement he unfurled the banner of imperialist expansion of which the canal would be a crucial element in the mix. What ties McKinley's words to those of Josiah Strong and anticipates the nationalist swagger of Albert Beveridge is an invocation of God's grace to sanction retention of the Philippines.

γ   γ   γ

Hold a moment longer! Not quite yet, gentlemen! Before you go I would like to say just a word about the Philippine business. I have been criticized a good deal about the Philippines, but don't deserve it. The truth is I didn't want the Philippines, and when they came to us, as a gift from the gods, I did not know what to do with them. When the Spanish War broke out [Admiral George] Dewey was at Hongkong, and I ordered him to go to Manila and to capture or destroy the Spanish fleet, and he had to; because, if defeated, he had no place to refit on that side of the globe, and if the Dons were victorious they would likely cross the Pacific and ravage our Oregon and California coasts. And so he had to destroy the Spanish fleet, and did it! But that was as far as I thought then.

When I next realized that the Philippines had dropped into our laps I confess I did not know what to do with them. I sought counsel from all sides—Democrats as well as Republicans—but got little help. I thought first we would take only Manila; then Luzon; then other islands perhaps also. I walked the floor of the White House night after night until midnight; and I am not ashamed to tell you, gentlemen, that I went down on my knees and prayed Almighty God for light and guidance more than one night. And one night late it came to me this way—I don't know how it was, but it came: (1) That we could not give them back to

* *Compilation of the Messages and Papers of Presidents* (Washington, D.C.: Government Printing Office, 1898), X, p. 180.

Spain—that would be cowardly and dishonorable; (2) that we could not turn them over to France and Germany—our commercial rivals in the Orient—that would be bad business and discreditable; (3) that we could not leave them to themselves—they were unfit for self-government—and they would soon have anarchy and misrule over there worse than Spain's was; and (4) that there was nothing left for us to do but to take them all, and to educate the Filipinos, and uplift and civilize and Christianize them, and by God's grace do the very best we could by them, as our fellow-men for whom Christ also died. And then I went to bed, and went to sleep, and slept soundly, and the next morning I sent for the chief engineer of the War Department (our map-maker), and I told him to put the Philippines on the map of the United States (pointing to a large map on the wall of his office), and there they are, and there they will stay while I am President!

DOCUMENT NO. 10

CONFIDENTIAL REACTION OF THE BRITISH MINISTRY TO THE FIRST HAY-PAUNCEFOTE TREATY*

In the wake of American victory in the Spanish-American War and United States presence in the Hawaiian Islands and the Philippines the prospect of an interoceanic canal became more definite. By 1899 it was evident to the London government that Washington was to go ahead with the project, if need be without British approval, and despite the provisions of the Clayton-Bulwer Treaty. It is useful therefore to consider some of the reactions in London to these developments. What may be inferred from this memorandum from the Board of Trade to the foreign secretary is that there will be an American-built canal and that the British must try to work out the best deal possible for its use.

γ   γ   γ

Board of Trade, *February 2, 1899*

Sir,

I AM directed by the Board of Trade to acknowledge the receipt of your letter of the 25th ultimo, inclosing a copy of a despatch from Her Majesty's Ambassador at Washington, transmitting a draft Convention supplemental to the Clayton-Bulwer Treaty.

With reference to your request to be furnished with the observations of the Board of Trade with regard to the matter, and also to the last paragraph of my letter of the 5th ultimo, I am directed to inclose, for Lord Salisbury's information, copy of a Memorandum and Statistical Tables with regard to the commercial aspects of the Nicaraguan Canal which have been prepared in this Department.

I am further directed to offer the following observations with regard to the terms of the draft Convention inclosed in your letter:—

1. Generally speaking, and subject to the observations made below, the Board of Trade see no objection to the provisions of the draft Convention on commercial grounds. The clause (Article II (1)) guaranteeing

* Foreign Office, File 55, p. 192.

equality of treatment appears to be amply sufficient to protect the interests of this country against differential treatment.

No doubt the interest of the United States in attracting vessels to the canal as well as their large interest in the actual trade and shipping passing through it (which is estimated by the Board of Trade at 46 per cent. in the case of the trade and 25 per cent. in the case of the shipping) may to a large extent be relied on to secure reasonable regulations and dues. On the other hand, as the main proprietors of the canal the Untied States may desire to keep the dues rather high, and the influence of the American railway interests is likely to be exercised in the same direction.

The Board of Trade have generally held that the Maritime Powers chiefly interested in a canal of this kind should, so far as possible, have some say as regards dues. In the present case their estimates lead them to suppose that of the shipping likely to pass the Nicaraguan Canal at the outset, about 47 per cent. will be engaged in trade to or from ports of the British Empire, and about 60 per cent. will carry the British flag. No further comment is necessary to show the magnitude of the interest of this country in the regulations and charges of the canal.

DOCUMENT NO. 11

WHITEHALL'S EVALUATION OF THE SECOND HAY-PAUNCEFOTE TREATY*

In the first year of the twentieth century it became even more clear the United States would go forward with a canal, either at Panama or across Nicaragua. The result was further pressure on the London government to give its approval, or at the very least to appear to do so, especially over the issue of a fortified canal. Two considerations stand out as crucial to British cooperation. One is the desire for an amicable solution; the second deals with the fortification issue.

γ   γ   γ

CONFIDENTIAL

Memorandum

Our refusal to accept the amendments inserted by the Senate in the Hay-Pauncefote Convention has led, as we anticipated, to a further proposal on the part of the United States' Government. I circulate, with an explanatory Memorandum by Mr. Villiers, a new draft Convention which Mr. Hay has prepared in consultation with a number of prominent Senators, and which Lord Pauncefote has been asked to submit to us privately in the first instance.

Lord Pauncefote's opinion may, I think, be summarized as follows:

He thinks the Senate would probably accept the new draft as it stands. He believes that an attempt to recast it would probably be fatal to its chance, and he inclines to the view that with one or two amendments which he suggests, the new addition might be accepted by His Majesty's Government.

We should, I believe, all of us be glad to find an amicable solution of this troublesome question. The conditions are, moreover, more favourable than they were, for whereas the inconsiderate action of the Senate last year justified us then in insisting on our strict rights and in pressing our objections to the utmost, it is open to us, now that we are approached in a very different spirit by Mr. Hay, to deal somewhat

* Foreign Office, File 55, p. 406.

less strictly with him so far as matters of form are concerned. We ought also to take into account the fact that Mr. Hay has laid before us not only this draft of a Convention relative to the construction of the Interoceanic Canal, but also a scheme for determining the Alaska boundary by arbitration, and a draft Treaty dealing with a number of the outstanding Canadian questions which we had hoped to settle in 1899, but which were left open by the Joint High Commission appointed in that year [*sic*].

On the other hand, however much we may desire an amicable settlement, it will be impossible for us to abandon abruptly the strong position which we took up in our despatch of the 22nd February, a despatch which was regarded with approval here, and was admitted in the United States to be a moderate and reasonable statement of the British Case.

(B.) *Reservation by the United States of the Right to Defend the Canal.*

To this amendment we objected very decidedly (see despatch [February 22, 1901], p. 3). The objectionable provision does not appear in the present draft, from which, however, is also omitted Rule 7 of Article II of the original Convention, under which the Contracting Parties were forbidden to fortify the canal. The two Rules were, as I pointed out at the time, antagonistic. I think we may be content to have them both omitted; but attention will, no doubt, be called to the omission of Rule 7, as suggesting that the right to fortify is not renounced.

The Rule against fortification was, I believe, of no practical value to us: the United State would not be likely to spend money on expensive works at the mouth of the canal or throughout its course, nor, if they did, would the control of the canal in time of war depend upon the presence or absence of such works.

DOCUMENT NO. 12

BRITAIN SEEKS TO PERSUADE CANADA TO ENDORSE THE HAY-HERBERT TREATY*

The deep suspicions the Canadian government had with respect to the Hay-Herbert Treaty intended to settle the Alaska boundary dispute in 1903 are well known and those suspicions were well grounded. Put bluntly the London government wanted the Canadians to sacrifice their interests in the cause of Anglo-American accord. What is interesting in this regard is the Foreign Office statement, urging Ottawa to give way. The date of the letter, February 23, 1903, is significant; shortly thereafter the Canadians agreed to accept a six man commission of arbitration and worse still, from their viewpoint, Roosevelt's appointees.

γ γ γ

His Majesty's Government were as much surprised as the Dominion Government at the selection of Mr. Elihu Root, and of Senators Lodge and Turner, to be the American members of the Tribunal, and cannot but feel, with the Canadian Government, that their appointment fails to fulfil in their complete sense the conditions laid down in Article I of the Convention.

The situation is full of difficulty, and His Majesty's Government earnestly desire to have the concurrence of the Canadian Government in dealing with it. It should, in their opinion, be borne in mind that the three gentlemen selected, all of them occupy conspicuous positions in the public life of the United States. A refusal to accept them as members of the Tribunal would unquestionably by greatly resented by the United States' Government, and by the American people generally.

It is true that the attitude of Senator Lodge has on various occasions been pronouncedly hostile to the Canadian contentions; but it is noteworthy that quite recently he took the leading part in disarming the hostility of the Senate towards the Treaty, and in bringing about its acceptance by that body.

Be this, however, as it may. His Majesty's Government are convinced that it would be of no avail to press the United States to withdraw the three names which they have put forward.

* *United States*, no. 1 (1904), pp. 45–46.

It would be easy to raise a discussion upon the fitness of the three American Representatives, but success in an argument of this nature would not only be barren of practical results, but would not improbably have the effect of sowing the seeds of lasting ill-will between the two countries.

His Majesty's Government are, therefore, virtually in the position of having to choose between, on the one hand, breaking off the negotiations altogether, or, on the other hand, accepting the American nominations, and appointing as their colleagues British Representatives appropriate to the altered circumstances of the case.

His Majesty's Government would regard the first alternative as a grave misfortune in the interests of both countries and of the Dominion of Canada. They would, in view of the restrictions under which the Tribunal is to carry out its work, prefer that the inquiry should proceed, in the confident expectation that it would not prejudice Canadian or British interests, while, even in case of failure, the result of its labours would probably be to collect much important information as to controverted points, and thereby to facilitate a reasonable settlement at some future time.

It would seem desirable that Lord Minto should urge his Ministers to weigh these considerations carefully. In the event of their sharing the opinion above expressed, His Majesty's Government hope that they will favour them with an expression of their views as to the manner in which the British side of the Tribunal might most advantageously be composed.

DOCUMENT NO. 13

TERMS OF THE ALASKA TRIBUNAL*

The portions of the rulings of the Tribunal recorded here leave no doubt that the American position of an even numbered tribunal membership and American contentions regarding the settlement of conflicting claims was exactly what Theodore Roosevelt wanted. The Tribunal was faced with a series of questions, seven in all. "A majority of the Tribunal, that is to say Lord Alverstone, Mr. Lodge, Mr. Root, and Mr. Turner" concurred in successive votes. The cut and dried character of the proceedings stands out, causing Canadians to experience deep resentment.

γ　　　　　　　γ　　　　　　　γ

Decision of the Alaskan Boundary Tribunal under the Treaty of January 24, 1903, between the United States and Great Britain

Whereas by a Convention signed at Washington on the 24th day of January 1903, by Plenipotentiaries of and on behalf of His Majesty the King of the United Kingdom of Great Britain and Ireland and of the British Dominions beyond the Seas, Emperor of India, and of and on behalf of the United States of America, it was agreed that a Tribunal should be appointed to consider and decide the questions hereinafter set forth, such Tribunal to consist of six impartial Jurists of repute, who should consider judicially the questions submitted to them each of whom should first subscribe an oath that he would impartially consider the arguments and evidence presented to the said Tribunal, and would decide thereupon according to his true judgment, and that three members of the said Tribunal should be appointed by His Britannic Majesty and three by the President of the United States:

In answer to the *first* question

The Tribunal unanimously agrees that the point of commencement of the line is Cape Muzon.

In answer to the *second* question

The Tribunal unanimously agrees that the Portland Channel is the Channel which runs from about 55° 56′ NL and passes to the north of Pearse and Wales Islands.

A majority of the Tribunal that is to say Lord Alverstone Mr Root

---

* *Treaties, 1776–1909*, Mallory, ed., I, pp. 792–94.

Mr Lodge and Mr Turner decides that the Portland Channel after passing to the north of Wales Island is the channel between Wales Island and Sitklan Island called Tongass Channel. The Portland Channel above mentioned is marked throughout its length by a dotted red line from the point B to the point marked C on the map signed in duplicate by the members of the Tribunal at the time of signing their decision.

In answer to the *third* question

A majority of the Tribunal that is to say Lord Alverstone Mr Root Mr Lodge and Mr Turner decides that the course of the line from the point of commencement to the entrance to Portland Channel is the line marked A B in red on the aforesaid map.

In answer to the *forth* question

A majority of the Tribunal that is to say Lord Alverstone Mr Root Mr Lodge and Mr Turner decides that the point to which the line is to be drawn from the head of the Portland Channel is the point on the 56th parallel of latitude marked D on the aforesaid map and the course which the line should follow is drawn from C to D on the aforesaid map.

In answer to the *fifth* question

A majority of the Tribunal, that is to say Lord Alverstone Mr Root Mr Lodge and Mr Turner decides that the answer to the above question is in the affirmative.

Question five having been answered in the affirmative question *six* requires no answer.

In answer to the *seventh* question

A majority of the Tribunal that is to say Lord Alverstone, Mr Root, Mr Lodge and Mr Turner decides that the mountains marked S on the aforesaid map are the mountains referred to as situated parallel to the coast on that part of the coast where such mountains marked S are situated and that between the points marked P (mountain marked S 8,000) on the north and the point marked T (mountain marked S 7,950) in the absence of further survey the evidence is not sufficient to enable the Tribunal to say which are the mountains parallel to the coast within the meaning of the Treaty.

In witness whereof we have signed the above written decision upon the questions submitted to us.

Signed in duplicate this twentieth day of October 1903.

ALVERSTONE
ELIHU ROOT
HENRY CABOT LODGE
GEORGE TURNER

DOCUMENT NO. 14

THEODORE ROOSEVELT ARTICULATES A COROLLARY TO THE MONROE DOCTRINE*

In a relatively few words President Roosevelt announced a major policy initiative regarding the United States as the premier power in the western hemisphere. He was convinced he was forced to do so by two debt crises, that of Venezuela (1902) and of the Dominican Republic (1904). It should be noted that the tone and the content of this portion of the president's annual message to Congress is balanced and moderate, and does not represent a saber rattling posture on the part of the United States. The key to Roosevelt's thinking is to be identified in the following statements: "Our interests and those of our southern neighbors are in reality identical." It is, in fact, a statesmanlike approach to problems in the Americas, a position he reiterated in his 1905 message to Congress.

γ   γ   γ

It is not true that the United States feels any land hunger or entertains any projects as regards the other nations of the Western Hemisphere save such as are for their welfare. All that this country desires is to see the neighboring countries stable, orderly, and prosperous. Any country whose people conduct themselves well can count upon our hearty friendship. If a nation shows that it knows how to act with reasonable efficiency and decency in social and political matters, if it keeps order and pays its obligations, it need fear no interference from the United States. Chronic wrongdoing, or an impotence which results in a general loosening of the ties of civilized society, may in America, as elsewhere, ultimately require intervention by some civilized nation, and in the Western Hemisphere the adherence of the United States to the Monroe Doctrine may force the United States, however reluctantly, in flagrant cases of such wrongdoing or impotence, to the exercise of an international police power. If every country washed by the Caribbean Sea would show the progress in stable and just civilization which with the aid of the Platt amendment Cuba has shown since our troops left the island, and which so many of the republics in both Americas are con-

---

* Roosevelt, Annual Message to Congress, December 1904, *Works* Memorial Edition, vol. 17, pp. 352–353.

stantly and brilliantly showing, all question of interference by this Nation with their affairs would be at an end. Our interests and those of our southern neighbors are in reality identical. They have great natural riches, and if within their borders the reign of law and justice obtains, prosperity is sure to come to them. While they thus obey the primary laws of civilized society they may rest assured that they will be treated by us in a spirit of cordial and helpful sympathy. We would interfere with them only in the last resort, and then only if it became evident that their inability or unwillingness to do justice at home and abroad had violated the rights of the United States or had invited foreign aggression to the detriment of the entire body of American nations. It is a mere truism to say that every nation, whether in America or anywhere else, which desires to maintain its freedom, its independence, must ultimately realize that the right of such independence can not be separated from the responsibility of making good use of it.

In asserting the Monroe Doctrine, in taking such steps as we have taken in regard to Cuba, Venezuela, and Panama, and in endeavoring to circumscribe the theater of war in the Far East, and to secure the open door in China, we have acted in our own interest as well as in the interest of humanity at large.

DOCUMENT NO. 15

W. W. ROCKHILL'S MEMORANDUM ON COMMERCIAL POLICY IN CHINA*

Few "memos" in the history of American diplomacy, as that diplomacy impacted on Great Britain, have had as much influence as that of W. W. Rockhill. It is the basis of the United States policy regarding China and the China trade as the new century dawned, and it set in motion events which would become reference points of Washington's China policy for many years to come. The memorandum also illustrates the fact that secretaries of state may enunciate plans while at the same time they are indebted to planners willing to give advice and transform their ideas into national commitments. The Open Door is formally the work of Secretary Hay, but no man is an island. And expert advice is likely to be persuasive if it points in the direction the head of the State Department wanted to go in the first place.

γ γ γ

No one person has done more within the last few months to influence public opinion in the United States on the Chinese question than Lord Charles Beresford, by his book "The Break-Up of China," and by the speeches he has made in the United States. By these means he has sought to prove the identity of interests of our two countries and the necessity of an Anglo-American policy in China. . . .

British writers on Chinese questions, and especially Lord Beresford, have advocated in the strongest terms the "open door policy" or equality of treatment and opportunity for all comers, and denounce in the strongest terms the system of "Spheres of Influence" (or interest); but such spheres have now been recognized by Great Britain as well as by France, Germany, and Russia, and *they must be accepted as existing facts.*

But while adopting the policy of spheres of interest, which, we will admit, political reasons may have forced it to do, Great Britain has tried to maintain also the "open door" policy, the only one which meets with the approval of its business classes, for by it alone can they be guaranteed equality of treatment in the trade of China. In this attempt to minimize the evils brought about by the necessities of her foreign policy, Great Britain has been, however, unable to secure to her people perfect

* *Foreign Relations* (1899), pp. 128–141.

equality of opportunity, for she has recognized special and exclusive rights first of Germany and then of Russia in their areas of activity, more particularly those relating to railways and mines. What these rights may eventually be claimed to include, no one can at present foretell, though it would not be surprising if the exercise of territorial jurisdiction and the imposition of discriminating taxation were demanded under them—at least by France. Should such rights be conceded, our trade interests would receive a blow, from which they could not possibly recover.

To sum up then, we find to-day in China that the policy of the "open door," the untrammeled exercise of the rights insured to Treaty Powers by the treaty of Tientsin, and other treaties copied on it or under the most favored nation clause, is claimed by the mercantile classes of the United States and other powers as essential to the healthy extension of trade in China. We see, on the other hand, that the political interests and the geographical relations of Great Britain, Russia and France to China have forced those countries to divide up China proper into areas or spheres of interest (or influence) in which they enjoy special rights and privileges, the ultimate scope of which is not yet determined, and that at the same time Great Britain, in its desire not to sacrifice entirely its mercantile interests, is also endeavoring to preserve some of the undoubted benefits of the "open door" policy, but "spheres of influence" *are an accomplished fact*, this cannot be too much insisted on. This policy is outlined by Mr. Balfour in his Manchester speech of January 10, 1898.

Such then being the condition of things, and in view of the probability of complications soon arising between the interested powers in China, whereby it will become difficult, if not impossible, for the United States to retain the rights guaranteed them by treaties with China, what should be our immediate policy? To this question there can, it seems, be but one answer, we should at once initiate negotiations to obtain from those Powers who have acquired zones of interest in China formal assurance that (1) they will in no way interfere within their so-called spheres of interest with any treaty port or with vested rights in it of any nature; (2) that all ports they may open in their respective spheres shall either be free ports, or that the Chinese treaty tariff at the time in force shall apply to all merchandise landed or shipped, no matter to what nationality belonging, and that the dues and duties provided for by treaty shall be collected by the Chinese Government; and (3) that they will levy no higher harbor dues on vessels of other nationalities frequenting their ports in such spheres than shall be levied on their national vessels, and that they will also levy no higher railroad charges on merchandise belonging to or destined for subjects of other powers transported through their spheres than shall be levied on similar merchandise belonging to its own nationality.

DOCUMENT NO. 16

THE FIRST OPEN DOOR NOTE*

Responding to the ideas of A. T. Mahan and Brooks Adams among others, and completely given over to the coming of age of the United States as a great power, John Hay issued the First Open Door Note in 1899. It has been referred to as a piece of Yankee bluff, the equivalent to asking all the thieves in a room to please stand up. Another way to view it, however, is as a cautious first step on Hay's part to test the water before proceeding further. Whatever the case it marks an extraordinary new departure in United States foreign policy.

γ   γ   γ

. . . Earnestly desirous to remove any cause of irritation and to insure at the same time to the commerce of all nations in China the undoubted benefits which should accrue from a formal recognition by the various powers claiming "spheres of influence" that they shall enjoy perfect equality of treatment for their commerce and navigation within such "spheres," the Government of the United States would be pleased to see His German Majesty's Government give formal assurances and lend its cooperation in securing like assurances from the other interested powers that each within its respective sphere of whatever influence—

First. Will in no way interfere with any treaty port or any vested interest within any so-called "sphere of interest" or leased territory it may have in China.

Second. That the Chinese treaty tariff of the time being shall apply to all merchandise within said "sphere of interest" (unless they be "free ports"), no matter to what nationality it may belong, and that duties so leviable shall be collected by the Chinese Government.

Third. That it will levy no higher harbor dues on vessels of another nationality frequenting any port in such "sphere" than shall be levied on vessels of its own nationality, and no higher railroad charges over lines built, controlled, or operated within its "sphere" on merchandise belonging to citizens or subjects of other nationalities transported

---

* *Treaties* Miller, David Hunter, ed. (Washington, D.C.: Government Printing Office, 1931) I, 549.

through such "sphere" than shall be levied on similar merchandise belonging to its own nationals transported over equal distances. . . .

The liberal policy pursued by His Imperial German Majesty in declaring Kiao-chao a free port and in aiding the Chinese Government in
the establishment there of a custom-house are so clearly in line with the
proposition which this Government is anxious to see recognized that it
entertains the strongest hope that Germany will give its acceptance and
hearty support.

The recent ukase of His Majesty the Emperor of Russia declaring
the port of Ta-lien-wan open during the whole of the lease under which
it is held from China to the merchant ships of all nations, coupled with
the categorical assurances made to this Government by His Imperial
Majesty's representative at this capital at the time and since repeated to
me by the present Russian ambassador, seem to insure the support of
the Emperor to the proposed measure. Our ambassador at the Court of
St. Petersburg has in consequence been instructed to submit it to the
Russian Government and to request their early consideration of it. A
copy of my instruction on the subject to Mr. Tower is herewith inclosed
for your confidential information.

The commercial interests of Great Britain and Japan will be so
clearly served by the desired declaration of intentions, and the views of
the Governments of these countries as to the desirability of the adoption
of measures insuring the benefits of equality of treatment of all foreign
trade throughout China are so similar to those entertained by the
United States, that their acceptance of the propositions herein outlined
and their cooperation in advocating their adoption by the other powers
can be confidently expected. . . .

In view of the present favorable conditions, you are instructed to
submit the above considerations to His Imperial German Majesty's
Minister for Foreign Affairs, and to request his early consideration of
the subject.

Copy of this instruction is sent to our ambassadors at London and at
St. Petersburg for their information.

DOCUMENT NO. 17

BRITISH REACTION TO THE FIRST OPEN DOOR NOTE*

The response of the Foreign Office must be described as a masterpiece of "contingent agreement." " . . . [P]rovided that a similar declaration is made by other powers" says it all.

γ   γ   γ

The British Reply

I have the honor to state that I have carefully considered, in communication with my colleagues, the proposal . . . that a declaration should be made by foreign powers claiming "spheres of interest" in China as to their intentions in regard to the treatment of foreign trade and interest therein.

I have much pleasure in informing your excellency that Her Majesty's Government will be prepared to make a declaration in the sense desired by your Government in regard to the leased territory of Wei-hai Wei and all territory in China which may hereafter be acquired by Great Britain by lease or otherwise, and all spheres of interest now held or that may hereafter be held by her in China, provided that a similar declaration is made by other powers concerned.

* *Foreign Relations*, 1899, pp. 129–130.

DOCUMENT NO. 18

THE SECOND OPEN DOOR NOTE*

In his enunciation of a Second Open Door Note Secretary Hay had moved from shallow water to deep water, where there might be encountered an unexpected undertow. The boldness of the last lines of the note continue to impress, almost one hundred years after the event. It is well to keep in mind that the McKinley administration was in power and that Hay shaped United States Far Eastern policy with the consent of "the first imperial president."

γ   γ   γ

In this critical posture of affairs in China it is deemed appropriate to define the attitude of the United States as far as present circumstances permit this to be done. We adhere to the policy initiated by us in 1857, of peace with the Chinese nation, of furtherance of lawful commerce, and of protection of lives and property of our citizens by all means guaranteed under extraterritorial treaty rights and by the law of nations. If wrong be done to our citizens we propose to hold the responsible authors to the uttermost accountability. We regard the condition at Pekin as one of virtual anarchy, whereby power and responsibility are practically devolved upon the local provincial authorities. So long as they are not in overt collusion with rebellion and use their power to protect foreign life and property we regard them as representing the Chinese people, with whom we seek to remain in peace and friendship. The purpose of the President is, as it has been heretofore, to act concurrently with the other powers, first, in opening up communication with Pekin and rescuing the American officials, missionaries, and other Americans who are in danger; secondly, in affording all possible protection everywhere in China to American life and property; thirdly, in guarding and protecting all legitimate American interests; and fourthly, in aiding to prevent a spread of the disorders to the other provinces of the Empire and a recurrence of such disasters. It is, of course, too early to forecast the means of attaining this last result; but the policy of the Government of the United States is to seek a solution which may bring

* *Foreign Relations*, 1900, p. 299.

about permanent safety and peace to China, preserve Chinese territorial and administrative entity, protect all rights guaranteed to friendly powers by treaty and international law, and safeguard for the world the principle of equal and impartial trade with all parts of the Chinese Empire.

DOCUMENT NO. 19

SPRING RICE ADVISES ROOSEVELT ON MATTERS OF WELTPOLITIK*

Spring Rice was not above lecturing the president on occasions, particularly when it came to thinking in terms of large policy. And Roosevelt was prepared to listen but not always to agree with Sir Cecil's arguments. It would be a mistake, nonetheless, not to recognize that the Englishman's outlook, always cogently expressed, filtered into his friend's evaluation of where and when Great Britain and the United States needed to be wary, and where and when they should stand together.

γ   γ   γ

I can't tell you how delightful it is to get such a letter from you and how glad I am to have such a friend. The world is not in very satisfactory condition and it is one firm pleasure at any rate to see a real man in the proper place for him, and to know that I know him.

I can't help thinking we are on the verge of great changes. What has happened here seems to be that the Emperor believed Japan was bluffing—was assured so by interested parties—and was encouraged by the war party and found it too late to retract. He absolutely refused to listen to his official councillor Lamsdorff and very often did not even tell him what had occurred.

Russia had been successful for many years in Asia in the policy of peaceful penetration—especially with England, who raised some ineffectual howls and ran; Japan had no question but one, that is Asia—and did not run. We spoiled Russia and she has to take the consequences. It is the firm conviction of Russia that the "Russian God" (an official expression) wills that Russia should occupy the whole of Asia; other nations are trespassers from overseas and have no rights. Treaties and engagements are temporary concessions in the weakness of the flesh, and must be got rid of when convenient. The point of view is that of a moral and religious right, supported by a feeling of innate conviction, and it is difficult to change. Japan was a mere trespasser in Corea, to be tolerated for a time and then removed. Treaty rights of foreigners were a temporary phase in the development of Asia which must disappear be-

* Spring Rice to Roosevelt, Feb. 1, 1904, Spring Rice Papers.

121

fore the light of dawning Russia. This is no exaggeration, it is the general and universally received opinion. It is Russia's strength and this conviction exists and is acted on with all the force of the national conscience.

That Japan should have dared resist is inconceivable; that she attacked when Russia was not ready, was monstrous. The explanation is—England and America. These friends of Japan incited her against holy and just Russia; and they must pay and be punished. America is far off and rather tough. England has the juicy and succulent morsel (India) within reach. So England can be made to pay and must pay. If this were all it wouldn't be a very serious matter. I quite agree with what you always said: England is where Englishmen can breed English children—not where millions of black men, sweltering in the sun, admire, prostrate, an Imperial Viceroy. I could support the loss of India with equanimity, if it did not mean the loss of a great free market, as well as the destruction, and hopeless destruction, of the work of two centuries. But what is that in the East?

DOCUMENT NO. 20

THE TAFT-KATSURA AGREEMENT (1905)*

All too often the Taft–Katsura Agreement is read solely in terms of American-Japanese relations. But in as much as Great Britain and Japan were formal allies and both nations were on friendly terms with the United States such an agreement amounted to a strengthening of the informal tie between London and Washington. One has only to recall how strongly Britain favored a sweeping Japanese victory to be able to appreciate a rejoicing in the Foreign Office that Washington and Tokyo were not likely to clash over their respective ambitions in the Far East.

γ   γ   γ

First, in speaking of some pro-Russians in America who would have the public believe that the victory of Japan would be a certain prelude to her aggression in the direction of the Philippine Islands, Secretary Taft observed that Japan's only interest in the Philippines would be, in his opinion, to have these islands governed by a strong and friendly nation like the United States. . . . Count Katsura confirmed in the strongest terms the correctness of his views on the point and positively stated that Japan does not harbor any aggressive designs whatever on the Philippines. . . .

Second, Count Katsura observed that the maintenance of general peace in the extreme East forms the fundamental principle of Japan's international policy. Such being the case, . . . the best, and in fact the only, means for accomplishing the above object would be to form good understanding between the three governments of Japan, the United States and Great Britain. . . .

Third, in regard to the Korean question Count Katsura observed that Korea being the direct cause of our war with Russia, it is a matter of absolute importance to Japan that a complete solution of the peninsula question should be made as the logical consequence of the war. If left to herself after the war, Korea will certainly draw back to her habit of improvidently entering into any agreements or treaties with other powers, thus resuscitating the same international complications as existed before the war. In view of the foregoing circumstances, Japan feels ab-

---

* *Miscellaneous Letters* of the Department of State, Part III, July 1905.

solutely constrained to take some definite step with a view to precluding the possibility of Korea falling back into her former condition and of placing us again under the necessity of entering upon another foreign war. Secretary Taft fully admitted the justness of the Count's observations and remarked to the effect that, in his personal opinion, the establishment by Japanese troops of a suzerainty over Korea to the extent of requiring that Korea enter into no foreign treaties without the consent of Japan was the logical result of the present war and would directly contribute to permanent peace in the East. His judgment was that President Roosevelt would concur in his views in this regard, although he had no authority to give assurance of this. . . .

DOCUMENT NO. 21

ROOT-TAKAHIRA AGREEMENT (1908)*

Few matters affecting its Far Eastern strategy would have pleased the British government more than the assurances contained in the Root-Takahira note. The status quo in that part of the world was to be maintained, at least to the point that the United States and Japan were able to bring this about. It struck the Foreign Office as real politik *at its more realistic: sane, workable, and respectful of spheres of influence all around. In short London was a beneficiary of the agreement, intentionally or otherwise.*

γ   γ   γ

Believing that a frank avowal of that aim, policy, and intention would not only tend to strengthen the relations of friendship and good neighborhood, which have immemorially existed between Japan and the United States, but would materially contribute to the preservation of the general peace, the Imperial Government have authorized me to present to you an outline of their understanding of that common aim, policy and intention:

1. It is the wish of the two Governments to encourage the free and peaceful development of their commerce on the Pacific Ocean.

2. The policy of both Governments, uninfluenced by any aggressive tendencies, is directed to the maintenance of the existing status quo in the region above mentioned and to the defense of the principle of equal opportunity for commerce and industry in China.

3. They are accordingly firmly resolved reciprocally to respect the territorial possessions belonging to each other in said region.

4. They are also determined to preserve the common interest of all powers in China by supporting by all pacific means at their disposal the independence and integrity of China and the principle of equal opportunity for commerce and industry of all nations in that Empire.

5. Should any event occur threatening the status quo as above described or the principle of equal opportunity as above defined, it remains for the two Governments to communicate with each other in order to arrive at an understanding as to what measures they may consider it useful to take. . . .

* *Foreign Relations,* 1908, pp. 511–512.

DOCUMENT NO. 22

ANGLO-AMERICAN
ARBITRATION TREATY (1908)*

*The closest the two countries came to full scale arbitration of differences
was in 1908. It is often referred to as a useful beginning in the process of
making wars between the English-speaking nations impossible, no matter how
sensitive the issues arising between them might be, including matters affecting
"national honor." The wording used therein indicates just how limited it
was: differences of a legal nature or relating to interpretations of treaty language. The arbitration treaty signed in 1914 simply extended the period of
years of these provisions, and as such fell well short of what President Taft
had sought from the Senate in 1912. Taft had proposed that "all differences
arising between the High Contracting Parties, which it has not been possible
to adjust by diplomacy, relating to international matters . . . shall be submitted to the Permanent Court of Arbitration established at The Hague.
. . . " The sticking point was this proposal stated that* all *differences be arbitrated.*

γ   γ   γ

The President of the United States of America and His Majesty the
King of the United Kingdom of Great Britain and Ireland and of the
British Dominions beyond the Seas, Emperor of India, desiring in pursuance of the principles set forth in Articles 15–19 of the Convention
for the pacific settlement of international disputes, signed at The Hague
July 29, 1899, to enter into negotiations for the conclusion of an Arbitration Convention, have named as their Plenipotentiaries, to wit:

The President of the United States of America, Elihu Root, Secretary of State of the United States, and

His Majesty the King of the United Kingdom of Great Britain and
Ireland and of the British Dominions beyond the Seas, Emperor of India, The Right Honorable James Bryce, O. M.,

who, after having communicated to one another their full powers,
found in good and due form, have agreed upon the following articles:

* *Foreign Relations*, 1908, pp. 510–511.

Article I

Differences which may arise of a legal nature or relating to the interpretation of treaties existing between the two Contracting Parties and which it may not have been possible to settle by diplomacy, shall be referred to the Permanent Court of Arbitration established at The Hague by the Convention of the 29th of July, 1899, provided, nevertheless, that they do not affect the vital interests, the independence, or the honor of the two Contracting States, and do not concern the interests of third Parties.

Article II

In each individual case the High Contracting Parties, before appealing to the Permanent Court of Arbitration, shall conclude a special Agreement defining clearly the matter in dispute, the scope of the powers of the Arbitrators, and the periods to be fixed for the formation of the Arbitral Tribunal and the several stages of the procedure. It is understood that such special agreements on the part of the United States will be made by the President of the United States, by and with the advice and consent of the Senate thereof; His Majesty's Government reserving the right before concluding a special agreement in any matter affecting the interests of a self governing Dominion of the British Empire to obtain the concurrence therein of the Government of that Dominion.

Such Agreements shall be binding only when confirmed by the two Governments by an Exchange of Notes.

Article III

The present Convention shall be ratified by the President of the United States of America by and with the advice and consent of the Senate thereof, and by his Britannic Majesty. The ratifications shall be exchanged at Washington as soon as possible, and the Convention shall take effect on the date of the exchange of its ratifications.

Article IV

The present Convention is concluded for a period of five years, dating from the day of the exchange of its ratifications.

Done in duplicate at the City of Washington, this fourth day of April, in the year 1908.

ELIHU ROOT   [SEAL]
JAMES BRYCE   [SEAL]

DOCUMENT NO. 23

PRESIDENT WILSON'S PROCLAMATION OF AMERICAN NEUTRALITY, AUGUST 1914*

When the guns of August began to boom the American public was caught unawares. It was perfectly natural for some people to choose sides: German-Americans favoring the old Fatherland and the eastern Establishment strongly pro-Allied. The vast majority of the plain people, however, were not so moved, preferring to remain "out of it." President Wilson urged his fellow citizens to be neutral in thought and in action and his message was well received by the majority, whether Democrat or Republican in their politics.

γ   γ   γ

The effect of the war upon the United States will depend upon what American citizens say and do. Every man who really loves America will act and speak in the true spirit of neutrality, which is the spirit of impartiality and fairness and friendliness to all concerned. The spirit of the nation in this critical matter will be determined largely by what individuals and society and those gathered in public meetings do and say, upon what newspapers and magazines contain, upon what ministers utter in their pulpits, and men proclaim as their opinions upon the street.

The people of the United States are drawn from many nations, and chiefly from the nations now at war. It is natural and inevitable that there should be the utmost variety of sympathy and desire among them with regard to the issues and circumstances of the conflict. Some will wish one nation, others another, to succeed in the momentous struggle. It will be easy to excite passion and difficult to allay it. Those reponsible for exciting it will assume a heavy responsibility, responsibility for no less a thing than that the people of the United States, whose love of their country and whose loyalty to its government should unite them as Americans all, bound in honor and affection to think first of her and her interests, may be divided in camps of hostile opinion, hot against each other, involved in the war itself in impulse and opinion if not in action.

Such divisions amongst us would be fatal to our peace of mind and might seriously stand in the way of the proper performance of our duty

---

* *Presidential Message to Congress*, 63rd Cong., 2nd Sess., Doc. No. 566.

as the one great nation at peace, the one people holding itself ready to play a part of impartial mediation and speak the counsels of peace and accommodation, not as a partisan, but as a friend.

I venture, therefore, my fellow countrymen, to speak a solemn word of warning to you against that deepest, most subtle, most essential breach of neutrality which may spring out of partisanship, out of passionately taking sides. The United States must be neutral in fact, as well as in name, during these days that are to try men's souls. We must be impartial in thought, as well as action, must put a curb upon our sentiments, as well as upon every transaction that might be construed as a preference of one party to the struggle before another.

DOCUMENT NO. 24

THE BRYCE REPORT*

The twentieth century witnessed the advent of organized propaganda agencies as integral parts of a nation's war machinery. And depending on how persuasive it was, propaganda could contribute directly to the outcome of the conflict. The British were ahead of the Germans: both countries bombarded the American public with information and disinformation of variety and imagination. But a common language, reenforced by so much common history, gave the British the advantage. The most notorious of these efforts at manipulating American public opinion was The Bryce Report. Its purpose was to expose the German soldiers as barbarian fiends: no atrocity was too horrible to attribute to them. But what made it plausible to many Americans was the name over which it was presented: Lord James Bryce, undoubtedly the most widely respected British official ever to serve in the United States.

γ   γ   γ

We saw the officer say something to the farmer's wife, and saw her push him away. After five or six minutes the two soldiers seized the woman and put her on the ground. She resisted them and they then pulled all her clothes off her until she was quite naked. The officer then violated her while one soldier held her by the shoulders and the other by the arms. After the officer each soldier in turn violated her, the other soldier holding her down. . . . After the woman had been violated by the three the officer cut off the woman's breasts.

We met a woman whose blouse or dress was torn open in front and she was all covered with blood. Her breasts had been cut off, the edges of the wounds being torn and rough. We spoke to the woman. She was with us for ten minutes, but it was impossible to understand what she was saying as she was *folle*.

One of the Germans took a rifle and struck her a tremendous blow with the butt on the head. Another took his bayonet and fixed it and thrust it through the child. He then put his rifle on his shoulder with the child up it, its little arms stretched out once or twice.

They were singing and making a lot of noise and dancing about. As the German soldiers came along the street I saw a small child, whether

* London: His Majesty's Stationers Office, 1915.

130

boy or girl I could not see, come out of a house. The child was about two years of age. The child came into the middle of the street so as to be in the way of the soldiers. The soldiers were walking in twos. The first line of two passed the child; one of the second line, the man on the left, stepped aside and drove his bayonet with both hands into the child's stomach, lifting the child into the air on his bayonet and carrying it away on his bayonet, he and his comrades still singing.

Immediately after the men had been killed, I saw the Germans going into the houses in the Place and bringing out the women and girls. About twenty were brought out. They were marched close to the corpses. Each of them was held by the arms. They tried to get away. They were made to lie on tables which had been brought into the square. About fifteen of them were then violated. Each of them was violated by about twelve soldiers. While this was going on about seventy Germans were standing round the women including five officers (young). The officers started it. There were some of the Germans between me and the women, but I could see everything perfectly. The ravishing went on for about one and one-half hours. I watched the whole time. Many of the women fainted and showed no sign of life. The Red Cross took them away to the hospital.

DOCUMENT NO. 25

"THE SHIP, THE FLAG, AND THE ENEMY"*

By early 1915 Americans were duly concerned by the methods used in the conduct of the war in so far as their neutral rights on the high seas were concerned. In a February 1915 issue of The Outlook, *a widely read journal of news and opinion, there appeared "The Ship, The Flag, and The Enemy" by Professor Ellery C. Stowell, a leading authority on international law. What he sought to do in his essay was to define terms in order to enable the public to come to a better understanding of America's rights, objectively considered. As the editor of* The Outlook *noted, Stowell was not advancing opinion but rather interpretation as he proceeded to answer a series of questions pertinent to the issues.*

γ   γ   γ

In the great conflict which is now going on, England, supreme on sea, and Germany, mightiest on land, have not been able to deal each other a vital blow. Their forces are deadlocked, and their Governments have recourse to indirect means to bring about a termination of the war. England has more funds for prolonging the contest, and hopes by using her credit and placing the burden on future generations to come to the end of Germany's resistance. Germany, on the other hand, relies on her magnificent organization to place on the shoulders of each individual a burden in proportion to what he has the strength to bear. This situation gives rise to many interesting questions, some of which I shall attempt to answer.

(1) *What is a war zone?*

If such a thing does exist, it certainly cannot be accurately defined. Perhaps it may be said to convey the idea of an area in which one or both of the belligerents find it necessary to exercise in the fullest measure their belligerent rights. The views of the belligerent in regard to the exercise of these rights may conflict with those of the neutral whose interests lie in protecting his commerce. The belligerent, to minimize the inconvenience to neutrals, may notify them of the date when such action will commence and of the area within which it will take place, expecting

* *The Outlook,* February 1915, pp. 392–393.

in return that the neutrals will be ready to allow without protest a fuller exercise of rights in accordance with his interpretation of them.

(2) *What is an effective blockade?*

An effective blockade is one that is maintained by a sufficient force to render dangerous the access to or egress from those ports or that portion of belligerent territory to which it is intended to apply. The London Declaration changed or simplified the diverse practices in regard to blockade. Although the rules of the Declaration of London do not constitute international law, it is to be expected that they will be applied except where a belligerent considers that he has a real interest to revert to his former practice. Whether a blockade can be maintained by means of floating mines or submarines is a disputed question of international law. The fundamental idea of a blockade is that it is a compromise between the right of neutrals to continue their ordinary commerce and the right of a belligerent to bring pressure to bear on his adversary by cutting off his trade with those ports or portions of his coast which he is able effectively to patrol by means of his naval force.

(3) *Has a belligerent a right to make use of torpedoes or other means to destroy his enemy's merchantmen, without visit and search, even though this may involve the death of passengers and crew?*

Without question a belligerent does not have any such right. The security of neutral commerce depends upon the strict observance of the rule which requires a belligerent to visit every ship and examine its papers before he seizes it or sinks it. In certain exceptional cases he may destroy a neutral vessel, liable to condemnation, when such action is necessary. Under no circumstances, however, whether the vessel be neutral or belligerent, may she be destroyed unless her papers are preserved and the safety of the passengers and crew provided for. No Government would for a moment maintain the right of its cruisers to fire and sink a vessel without a previous visit and examination of the ship's papers. The fact that a shot is delivered below the surface of the water does not in the slightest affect this principle. It is not a sufficient compliance with the requirements for the safety of the passengers and crew to turn them adrift in small boats. Should loss of life result from this action to any American citizen it would be good ground for war.

DOCUMENT NO. 26

WILSON'S THIRD *LUSITANIA* NOTE, JULY 1915*

President Wilson utilized the most restrained language in protesting the destruction of unarmed shipping. It is difficult to construe it as an ultimatum except for the fact it was a formal transmission of what was both American policy and American fear of worse to come. Yet it shook up the State Department to the extent it helped bring about the resignation of Secretary of State Bryan. A mincing of words perhaps but one of many protests about the sea war as fought by both Britain and Germany.

γ   γ   γ

The note of the Imperial German Government, dated July 8, 1915, has received the careful consideration of the Government of the United States, and it regrets to be obliged to say that it has found it very unsatisfactory, because it fails to meet the real differences between the two Governments and indicates no way in which the accepted principles of law and humanity may be applied in the grave matter in controversy, but proposes, on the contrary, arrangements for a partial suspension of those principles which virtually set them aside.

The Government of the United States notes with satisfaction that the Imperial German Government recognizes without reservation the validity of the principles insisted on in the several communications which this Government has addressed to the Imperial German Government with regard to its announcement of a war zone and the use of submarines against merchantmen on the high seas—the principle that the high seas are free, that the character and cargo of a merchantman must first be ascertained before she can lawfully be seized or destroyed, and that the lives of non-combatants may in no case be put in jeopardy unless the vessel resists or seeks to escape after being summoned to submit to examination; for a belligerent act of retaliation is *per se* an act beyond the law, and the defense of an act as retaliatory is an admission that it is illegal.

* *Papers of Woodrow Wilson* (Princeton, N.J.: Princeton University Press, 1980) vol. 33, July 15, 1915, pp. 530–532.

The Government of the United States is, however, keenly disappointed to find that the Imperial German Government regards itself as in large degree exempt from the obligation to observe these principles, even where neutral vessels are concerned, by what it believes the policy and practice of the Government of Great Britain to be in the present war with regard to neutral commerce. The Imperial German Government will readily understand that the Government of the United States can not discuss the policy of the Government of Great Britain with regard to neutral trade except with that Government itself, and that it must regard the conduct of other belligerent governments as irrelevant to any discussion with the Imperial German Government of what this Government regards as grave and unjustifiable violations of the rights of American citizens by German naval commanders. Illegal and inhuman acts, however justifiable they may be thought to be against an enemy who is believed to have acted in contravention of law and humanity, are manifestly indefensible when they deprive neutrals of their acknowledged rights, particularly when they violate the right to life itself. If a belligerent can not retaliate against an enemy without injuring the lives of neutrals, as well as their property, humanity, as well as justice and a due regard for the dignity of neutral powers, should dictate that the practice be discontinued. If persisted in, it would in such circumstances constitute an unpardonable offense against the sovereignty of the neutral nation affected. The Government of the United States is not unmindful of the extraordinary conditions created by this war or of the radical alterations of circumstance and method of attack produced by the use of instrumentalities of naval warfare which the nations of the world can not have had in view when the existing rules of international law were formulated, and it is ready to make every reasonable allowance for these novel and unexpected aspects of war at sea; but it can not consent to abate any essential or fundamental right of its people because of a mere alteration of circumstance. The rights of neutrals in time of war are based upon principle, not upon expediency, and the principles are immutable. It is the duty and obligation of belligerents to find a way to adapt the new circumstances to them.

In view of the admission of illegality made by the Imperial Government when it pleaded the right of retaliation in defense of its acts, and in view of the manifest possibility of conforming to the established rules of naval warfare, the Government of the United States can not believe that the Imperial Government will longer refrain from disavowing the wanton act of its naval commander in sinking the *Lusitania* or from offering reparation for the American lives lost, so far as reparation can be made for a needless destruction of human life by an illegal act.

DOCUMENT NO. 27

PROTEST OVER THE BLACKLIST, 1916*

*Few if any actions by the British government that affected the rights of
neutrals to trade openly was more resented in the United States than the
"blacklist." There were good reasons for the American reaction. Not only did
it appear to be a matter of extortion but there was the further fear that the
British would make use of it once the war was over. In this way their peacetime merchant marine would benefit as American firms and shippers were
proscribed, a sword cutting two ways.*

γ   γ   γ

The announcement that His Britannic Majesty's Government has
placed the names of certain persons, firms, and corporations in the
United States upon a proscriptive 'black list', and has forbidden all financial or commercial dealings between them and citizens of Great
Britain, has been received with the most painful surprise by the people
and Government of the United States, and seems to the Government
of the United States to embody a policy of arbitrary interference with
neutral trade against which it is its duty to protest in the most decided
terms.

The scope and effect of the policy are extraordinary. British steamship companies will not accept cargoes from the proscribed firms or
persons or transport their goods to any port, and steamship lines under
neutral ownership understand that if they accept freight from them they
are likely to be denied coal at British ports and excluded from other
privileges which they have usually enjoyed and may themselves be put
upon the black list. Neutral bankers refuse loans to those on the list and
neutral merchants decline to contract for their goods, fearing a like proscription. It appears that British officials regard the prohibitions of the
black list as applicable to domestic commercial transactions in foreign
countries as well as in Great Britain and her dependencies, for Americans doing business in foreign countries have been put on notice that
their dealings with blacklisted firms are to be regarded as subject to veto
by the British Government. By the same principle, Americans in the
United States might be made subject to similar punitive action if they

* *Foreign Relations,* 1916, Supplement, pp. 411–424.

were found dealing with any of their own countrymen whose names had thus been listed.

The harsh and even disastrous effects of this policy upon the trade of the United States, and upon the neutral rights upon which it will not fail to insist, are obvious. Upon the list of those proscribed and in effect shut out from the general commerce of the world may be found American concerns which are engaged in large commercial operations as importers of foreign products and materials and as distributors of American products and manufacturers to foreign countries, and which constitute important channels through which American trade reaches the outside world. Their foreign affiliations may have been fostered for many years, and when once broken cannot easily or promptly be reestablished. Other concerns may be put upon the list at any time and without notice. It is understood that additions to the proscription may be made 'whenever on account of enemy nationality or enemy association of such persons or bodies of persons it appears to His Majesty expedient to do so'. The possibilities of undeserved injury to American citizens from such measures, arbitrarily taken, and of serious and incalculable interruptions of American trade are without limit.

It has been stated on behalf of His Majesty's Government that these measures were aimed only at the enemies of Great Britain and would be adopted and enforced with strict regard to the rights of neutrals and with the least possible detriment to neutral trade, but it is evident that they are inevitably and essentially inconsistent with the rights of the citizens of all the nations not involved in war. The Government of the United States begs to remind the Government of His Britannic Majesty that citizens of the United States are entirely within their rights in attempting to trade with the people or the governments of any of the nations now at war, subject only to well-defined international practices and understandings which the Government of the United States deems the Government of Great Britain to have too lightly and too frequently disregarded.

DOCUMENT NO. 28

THE HOUSE-GREY MEMORANDUM, 1916*

Much is made of this memorandum, agreed to between someone who was an informal spokesman for the American chief executive and the British foreign secretary who was, of course, answerable to the War Cabinet. However sincere the purpose of Colonel House, whose initiative brought it about, it was akin to spitting in the wind. Neither the Allies nor the Central Powers were prepared to stop the fighting, witness the battle of the Somme later that year.

γ   γ   γ

'(*Confidential*)

'Colonel House told me that President Wilson was ready, on hearing from France and England that the moment was opportune, to propose that a Conference should be summoned to put an end to the war. Should the Allies accept this proposal, and should Germany refuse it, the United States would probably enter the war against Germany.

'Colonel House expressed the opinion that, if such a Conference met, it would secure peace on terms not unfavourable to the Allies; and, if it failed to secure peace, the United States would leave the Conference as a belligerent on the side of the Allies, if Germany was unreasonable. Colonel House expressed an opinion decidedly favourable to the restoration of Belgium, the transfer of Alsace and Lorraine to France, and the acquisition by Russia of an outlet to the sea, though he thought that the loss of territory incurred by Germany in one place would have to be compensated to her by concessions to her in other places outside Europe. If the Allies delayed accepting the offer of President Wilson, and if, later on, the course of the war was so unfavourable to them that the intervention of the United States would not be effective, the United States would probably disinterest themselves in Europe and look to their own protection in their own way.

'I said that I felt the statement, coming from the President of the United States, to be a matter of such importance that I must inform the Prime Minister and my colleagues; but that I could say nothing until it had received their consideration. The British Government could, under

* *The Intimate Papers of Colonel House* 4 vols., Charles Seymour, ed. (Boston and New York: Houghton Mifflin Company, 1926) II, pp. 203–204.

no circumstances, accept or make any proposal except in consultation and agreement with the Allies. I thought that the Cabinet would probably feel that the present situation would not justify them in approaching their Allies on this subject at the present moment; but, as Colonel House had had an intimate conversation with M. Briand and M. Jules Cambon in Paris, I should think it right to tell M. Briand privately, through the French Ambassador in London, what Colonel House had said to us; and I should, of course, whenever there was an opportunity, be ready to talk the matter over with M. Briand, if he desired it.'

DOCUMENT NO. 29

PRESIDENT WILSON'S SUSSEX
ULTIMATUM, 1916*

Woodrow Wilson was a man of peace; he looked upon the use of military power to gain his objectives as the very last resort. Therefore, upon news of the sinking of the French cross-channel steamer the Sussex *he wrote in the strongest terms possible to denounce the sinking and to demand a cessation of German unrestricted submarine warfare. It was the tone and the content of his protest, part of which appears here, that persuaded the German High Command to forego all out submarine attacks. Wilson was euphoric, not alone because he believed lives would be saved but also because as a man of peace the pen appeared to be mightier than the sword.*

γ   γ   γ

Information now in the possession of the Government of the United States fully establishes the facts in the case of the *Sussex*, and the inferences which my Government has drawn from that information it regards as confirmed by the circumstances set forth in your excellency's note of the 10th instant. On the 24th of March 1916, at about 2.50 o'clock in the afternoon, the unarmed steamer *Sussex*, with 325 or more passengers on board, among whom were a number of American citizens, was torpedoed while crossing from Folkestone to Dieppe. The *Sussex* had never been armed; was a vessel known to be habitually used only for the conveyance of passengers across the English Channel; and was not following the route taken by troopships or supply ships. About 80 of her passengers, non-combatants of all ages and sexes, including citizens of the United States, were killed or injured.

A careful, detailed, and scrupulously impartial investigation by naval and military officers of the United States has conclusively established the fact that the *Sussex* was torpedoed without warning or summons to surrender and that the torpedo by which she was struck was of German manufacture. In the view of the Government of the United States these facts from the first made the conclusion that the torpedo was fired by a German submarine unavoidable. It now considers that conclusion substantiated by the statements of your excellency's note. A full statement

* *Foreign Relations*, 1916, Supplement, pp. 232–234.

of the facts upon which the Government of the United States has based
its conclusion is enclosed.

In pursuance of this policy of submarine warfare against the commerce of its adversaries, thus announced and thus entered upon in despite of the solemn protest of the Government of the United States, the
commanders of the Imperial Government's undersea vessels have carried on practices of such ruthless destruction which have made it more
and more evident as the months have gone by that the Imperial Government has found it impracticable to put any such restraints upon them
as it had hoped and promised to put. Again and again the Imperial Government has given its solemn assurances to the Government of the
United States that at least passenger ships would not be thus dealt with,
and yet it has repeatedly permitted its undersea commanders to disregard those assurances with entire impunity. As recently as February last
it gave notice that it would regard all armed merchantmen owned by its
enemies as part of the armed naval forces of its adversaries and deal with
them as with men-of-war, thus, at least by implication, pledging itself
to give warning to vessels which were not armed and to accord security
of life to their passengers and crews; but even this limitation its submarine commanders have recklessly ignored.

If it is still the purpose of the Imperial Government to prosecute re-
lentless and indiscriminate warfare against vessels of commerce by the
use of submarines without regard to what the Government of the
United States must consider the sacred and indisputable rules of international law and the universally recognized dictates of humanity, the
Government of the United States is at last forced to the conclusion that
there is but one course it can pursue. Unless the Imperial Government
should now immediately declare and effect an abandonment of its present methods of submarine warfare against passenger and freight-carry-
ing vessels, the government of the United States can have no choice but
to sever diplomatic relations with the German Empire altogether. This
action the Government of the United States contemplates with the
greatest reluctance but feels constrained to take in behalf of humanity
and the rights of neutral nations.

DOCUMENT NO. 30

ZIMMERMANN TELEGRAM, 1917*

This telegram was sent by the German foreign secretary, Alfred Zimmermann, to Baron von Eckhardt, German minister to Mexico, dated January 19, 1917. Held by British Intelligence for some weeks, it was received at the State Department, March 1. It has to be characterized as one of the most provocative yet maladroit pieces of communication in the history of wartime diplomacy. It reveals in the German foreign secretary an ignorance of American psychology and an indifference to American public opinion inviting disaster.

γ　　　　　　γ　　　　　　γ

We intend to begin on the 1st of February unrestricted submarine warfare. We shall endeavor in spite of this to keep the United States of America neutral. In the event of this not succeeding, we make Mexico a proposal of alliance on the following basis: make war together, make peace together, generous financial support and an understanding on our part that Mexico is to reconquer the lost territory in Texas, New Mexico, and Arizona. The settlement in detail is left to you. You will inform the President of the above most secretly as soon as the outbreak of war with the United States of America is certain and add the suggestion that he should, on his own initiative, invite Japan to immediate adherence and at the same time mediate between Japan and ourselves. Please call the President's attention to the fact that the ruthless employment of our submarines now offers the prospect of compelling England in a few months to make peace.

* *Foreign Relations*, 1917, Supplement I, pp. 147–148.

DOCUMENT NO. 31

PRESIDENT WILSON'S WAR
MESSAGE, APRIL 1917*

The climax of British-American diplomacy took the form of the American president calling upon Congress to declare way against Germany and its Allies, thereby associating the United States with the Allied cause, with Great Britain in particular. As eager as the French may have been for the United States to come into the war it was the diplomatic exchanges between the two English-speaking nations that facilitated, and in some ways, forced the issue.

γ   γ   γ

On the third of February last I officially laid before you the extraordinary announcement of the Imperial German Government that on and after the first day of February it was its purpose to put aside all restraints of law of humanity and use its submarines to sink every vessel that sought to approach either the ports of Great Britain and Ireland or the western coasts of Europe or any of the ports controlled by the enemies of Germany within the Mediterranean. That had seemed to be the object of the German submarine warfare earlier in the war, but since April of last year the Imperial Government had somewhat restrained the commanders of its undersea craft in conformity with its promise then given to us that passenger boats should not be sunk and that due warning would be given to all other vessels which its submarines might seek to destroy, when no resistance was offered or escape attempted, and care taken that their crews were given at least a fair chance to save their lives in their open boats. The precautions taken were meagre and haphazard enough, as was proved in distressing instance after instance in the progress of the cruel and unmanly business, but a certain degree of restraint was observed. The new policy has swept every restriction aside. Vessels of every kind, whatever their flag, their character, their cargo, their destination, their errand, have been ruthlessly sent to the bottom without warning and without thought of help or mercy for those on board, the vessels of friendly neutrals along with those of belligerents. Even hospital ships and ships carrying relief to the sorely bereaved and

* *Public Papers of Woodrow Wilson*, vol. 4, pp. 422–426.

stricken people of Belgium, though the latter were provided with safe conduct through the proscribed areas by the German Government itself and were distinguished by unmistakable marks of identity, have been sunk with the same reckless lack of compassion or of principle.

With a profound sense of the solemn and even tragical character of the step I am taking and of the grave responsibilities which it involves, but in unhesitating obedience to what I deem my constitutional duty, I advise that the Congress declare the recent course of the Imperial German Government to be in fact nothing less than war against the government and people of the United States; that it formally accept the status of belligerent which has thus been thrust upon it; and that it take immediate steps not only to put the country in a more thorough state of defense but also to exert all its power and employ all its resources to bring the Government of the German Empire to terms and end the war.

. . .

It is a distressing and oppressive duty, Gentlemen of the Congress, which I have performed in thus addressing you. There are, it may be, many months of fiery trial and sacrifice ahead of us. It is a fearful thing to lead this great peaceful people into war, into the most terrible and disastrous of all wars, civilization itself seeming to be in the balance. But the right is more precious than peace, and we shall fight for the things which we have always carried nearest our hearts—for democracy, for the right of those who submit to authority to have a voice in their own governments, for the rights and liberties of small nations, for a universal dominion of right by such a concert of free peoples as shall bring peace and safety to all nations and make the world itself at last free. To such a task we can dedicate our lives and our fortunes, everything that we are and everything that we have, with the pride of those who know that the day has come when America is privileged to spend her blood and her might for the principles that gave her birth and happiness and the peace which she has treasured. God helping her, she can do no other.

BIBLIOGRAPHY

Allen, H. C. *Great Britain and the United States,* (New York: St. Martin's Press, 1955)

Bailey, Thomas A., *Theodore Roosevelt and the Japanese-American Crises,* (Stanford, CA: Stanford University Press, 1934)

Beale, Howard K., *Theodore Roosevelt and the Rise of America to World Power,* (Baltimore: Johns Hopkins University Press, 1956)

Burton, David H., *Theodore Roosevelt Confident Imperialist,* (Philadelphia: University of Pennsylvania Press, 1969)

Burton, David H., *Theodore Roosevelt and his English Correspondents,* (Philadelphia: American Philosophical Society, 1972)

Campbell, A. E., *Great Britain and the United States, 1895–1903,* (London: Longmans, 1960)

Campbell, C. S., *Anglo-American Understanding, 1898–1902,* (Baltimore: Johns Hopkins University Press, 1957)

Cooper, John M., *The Vanity of Power,* (Westport, CT, Greenwood Press, 1969)

Cooper, John M., *Walter Hines Page, Southerner as American,* (Chapel Hill, University of North Carolina Press, 1977)

Dennett, Tyler, *John Hay From Poetry to Politics,* (New York: Dodd, Mead, 1933)

Dennett, Tyler, *Theodore Roosevelt and the Russo-Japanese War,* (Garden City, NY: Doubleday Page, 1925)

Devlin, Patrick, *Too Proud To Fight,* (London: Oxford University Press, 1974)

Dobson, Alan P., *Anglo-American Relations in the 20th Century,* (New York: Routledge, 1995)

Dulles, Foster Rhea, *The Imperial Years,* (New York: Crowell, 1956)

Esthus, Raymond A., *Theodore Roosevelt and Japan,* (Seattle: University of Washington Press, 1966)

Ferguson, Thomas F., *American Diplomacy and the Boer War,* (Philadelphia: University of Pennsylvania Press, 1939)

Garvin, John and Amery, Julien, *The Life of Joseph Chamberlain,* 4 vols., (London: Macmillan, 1951)

Gassett, Thomas P., *Race: The History of an Idea in America,* (Dallas: Southern Methodist University Press, 1963)

George, Alexander and Juliet, *Woodrow Wilson and Colonel House: A Personality Study,* (New York: J. Day, 1956)

Grenville, John A. S., *Lord Salisbury and Foreign Policy,* (London: University of London Press, 1964)

Griswold, A. Whitney, *The Far Eastern Policy of the United States,* (New Haven, CT: Yale University Press, 1938)

Harbaugh, W. H., *Power and Personality The Life of Theodore Roosevelt*, (New York: Collier, 1963)

Heindel, Richard H., *The American Impact on Great Britain, 1898–1914*, (New York: Octogan Books, 1968)

Hendricks, Burton K., *The Life and Letters of Walter Hines Page*, 3 vols. (Garden City: Doubleday, Page, 1922–1925)

Kennan, George, *American Diplomacy 1900–1950*, (London: Secker and Warburg, 1952)

Lafeber, Walter, *The New Empire*, (Ithaca, NY: Cornell University Press, 1963)

Langer, William L., *The Diplomacy of Imperialism*, 2 vols., (New York: Knopf, 1950)

Link, Arthur, *Wilson: The Diplomatist*, (New York: New Viewpoints, 1974)

Link, Arthur, *Wilson: The Struggle for Neutrality*, (Princeton, NJ: Princeton University Press, 1960)

May, Earnest, R., *Imperial Democracy*, (New York: Harcourt Brace, 1961)

May, Henry F., *The End of American Innocence*, (Chicago: Quadrangle, 1959)

Millis, Walter, *The Road to War, 1914–1917*, (London: Faber, 1935)

Mowat, R. B., *The Life of Lord Pauncefote*, (London: Constable, 1929)

Munro, Dana G., *Intervention: Dollar Diplomacy in the Caribbean*, (Princeton, NJ: Princeton University Press, 1964)

Neale, R. G., *Great Britain and United States Expansion*, (East Lansing: Michigan State University Press, 1966)

Neu, Charles, *Theodore Roosevelt and Japan: An Uncertain Friendship*, (Cambridge, MA: Harvard University Press, 1967)

Nevins, Allan, *Henry White: Thirty Years of American Diplomacy*, (New York: Harper Brothers, 1930)

Nish, Ian, *The Anglo-Japanese Alliance*, (London: University of London Press, 1966)

Netter, Harley, *The Origins of the Foreign Policy of Woodrow Wilson*, (Baltimore: Johns Hopkins University Press, 1937)

Osgood, Robert E., *Ideals and Self-Interest in American Foreign Policy*, (Chicago: University of Chicago Press, 1953)

Perkins, Bradford, *The Great Rapprochement England and the United States, 1895–1914*, (New York: Atheneum, 1968)

Perkins, Dexter, *The Monroe Doctrine, 1867–1907*, (Baltimore: Johns Hopkins University Press, 1937)

Peterson, Harold C., *Propaganda For War*, (Norman: University of Oklahoma Press, 1939)

Russett, Bruce M., *Community and Contention: Britain and America in the Twentieth Century*, (Cambridge: Massachusetts Institute of Technology Press, 1963)

Seymour, Charles, *American Neutrality, 1914-1917*, (New Haven: Yale University Press, 1935)

Smith, Tony, *Patterns of Imperialism*, (Cambridge: Cambridge University Press, 1981)

Stead, W. T., *The Americanisation of the World*, (London: Review of Reviews, 1902)

Tansill, Charles Callin, *America Goes To War*, (Boston: Little Brown, 1938)

Tansill, Charles Callin, *Canadian-American Relations, 1875-1911*, (New Haven, CT: Yale University Press, 1943)

Tansill, Charles Callin, *The Foreign Policy of Thomas F. Bayard*, (New York: Fordham University Press, 1940)

Tilchin, William, *Theodore Roosevelt and the British Empire*, (New York: St. Martin's Press, 1997)

Trevelyan, George M., *Grey of Fallodon*, 2 vols., (Boston: Houghton Mifflin, 1937)

Varg, Paul, *Open Door Diplomacy: The Life of W. W. Rockhill*, (Urbana: University of Illinois Press, 1952)

Wienberg, Albert K., *Manifest Destiny*, (Baltimore: Johns Hopkins University Press, 1964)

Young, George B., *Politics, Strategy and American Diplomacy*, (New Haven, CT: Yale University Press, 1966)

INDEX